1

THE ORIGINAL

FAIRHOPE GUIDEBOOK

Second Edition

Fairhope Writers Group

The Original Fairhope Guidebook

Published by the Fairhope Writers Group. For further
information concerning the authors' availability, contact Ron
Meszaros at Page and Palette Bookstore, Fairhope, Alabama.
251-928-5295 or Email: ronmeszaros@yahoo.com. Follow us on
Facebook, The Fairhope Writers Group.

Cover design and artwork by Ellen Grigg.
Black and white photography by Ron Meszaros and Jerome
Cartier (unless otherwise noted).

ISBN-9781698569390

Second Edition

PRINTED IN THE UNITED STATES OF AMERICA

Our Town

No city, town, village, or community stands still. They are forever growing and shrinking and creating new identities for themselves every day, unnoticed by the inhabitants. This is our little town. While we have endeavored to capture the truth and the spirit of Fairhope, Alabama, that would be an impossible task and would require a thousand pages. This, then, is a snapshot taken over several months by a group of writers who live and enjoy life here. We may have missed something here and there, but we consider that a part of our town's charm. There always will be something hidden out there, and we hope you consider whatever you find your own personal discovery.

Our Book

Do not expect a dry, boring, "just-the-facts, ma'am" presentation in this "Original" guidebook. We are all creative writers, and take the word "original" very seriously. Our various muses disallowed, for the most part, a purely journalistic rendition. While you will find facts and honest reviews, they are liberally sprinkled with whimsy, fun, and a few prevarications to, we hope, make your stay in Fairhope even more enjoyable. We don't proclaim this to be a comprehensive compilation. There are just too many places to go, people to see, and things to do—and changes going on—to think we can do justice to everything. So, if your favorite place isn't in here, don't feel slighted. Maybe next time.

The Original Fairhope Guidebook

Table of Contents

Dragonfly Foodbar
Fairhope Inn and Restaurant
Honeybaked Ham
It's All Greek to Me
Julwin's Café
Little Whiskey Christmas Club
Locals
Mary Ann's Deli
Master Joe's
McSharry's Irish Pub
Mill, The
    Cereal Killer
    Ox Kitchen
    Sundae School
    Taps
Panini Pete's
R Bistro and Bakery
Ravenite
Sage Lebanese Cuisine and Café
Sandra's Place Deli
Section Street Pizza
Tamara's Downtown
Texarbama BBQ
Thyme on Section
Wok By d'Day

Christmas Round the Corner
Church Mouse
Living Well
Ole Bay Mercantile
The Picture Show
Poppins
River Bend

Brennys Jewelry

Brennys Too
Stowe's Jewelers
Wismar

Adrenaline
B Southern
CK Collections
CK Collection Men's
Cat's Meow
The Colony Shop
Cybele's
East Bay Clothiers
Fairhope Store, The
Four Bags
GiGi & Jay's
LaRobe
The Little Drawer
Le Papillion
M & F Casuals
Ooh La La
Private Gallery
Rush
Sadie's
Seven South
Shoefly
Southern Gents
Stephanie's
Sway
Tiny Town
Utopia
Vine

Back on the Rack
Hertha's Second Edition
Revolution Resale

Eastern Shore Art Center

Lakewood Golf Course (Marriott Grand)
Quail Creek Golf Course (City Course)
Rock Creek Golf Course (Private/Public)
Let's Exercise
Pro Cycle and Tri
Sitting

How the Fairhope Annual Arts and Crafts

Eastern Shore Repertory Theatre
First Friday Art Walk
Let the Celebrations Commence
    New Year's Eve
    Theatre 98
    Mardi Gras
    Annual Arts and Craft Show
    Earth Day
    Girls' Night Out
    Farmer's Market
    Baldwin Pops Concerts
    Book Festival
    Birdfest
    Film Festival
    Christmas Lighting of Trees
    Christmas Parade
Live at Five (A Concert Series in Fairhope)

Grand Hotel Marriott Resort
Hampton Inn
Jubilee Suites
Bay Breeze Guest House
Cottages of Fairhope
Emma's Bay House
Fairhope Inn
Baron's by the Bay Inn

Holiday Inn Express

Lagniappe *A Cajun term for "a little something extra"*

Not in Walking Distance, but Worth a Short Drive

Agave Cocina Mexicana and Tequila Bar
Coffee Loft
El Mexicano
Fairhope Brewing Company
Fairhope Roasting Company
Gambino's Italian Grill
Grand Hotel Restaurants
Lickin' Good Donut Shop
Rotolo's
Sunset Pointe
Tokyo Sushi & Hibachi
Warehouse Bakery and Donuts
Washhouse Restaurant
Yak, the Kathmandu Kitchen
Fairhope Furniture Consignment
The Silver Market
Joyce's Hair Salon

Welcome to Fairhope

Photo by Robert M. Glennon

Whether you are regular visitors, new residents, or have just stumbled across Fairhope in your travels, we are sure you have noticed that there is something special about this little spot on Mobile Bay.

The fact that its inception more than 100 years ago was as a Utopian experiment may have had lingering influence as it slowly evolved into what it is today. Fairhope has been described as a step back in time, Mayberry by the bay, and small town Americana as Norman Rockwell would have painted it.

It's quaint, artsy, picturesque, and brimming with non-glitzy things to do and see. There are a wealth of specialty shops and family-friendly events to meet all needs and please all interests. A nearly 1,500-foot pier invites fishing, walking, or simply savoring the Bay breeze. There are walking trails and bicycle lanes. Culinary delights abound, and the multitude of delightful flower beds and hanging baskets in all seasons just make your eyes smile. And, oh, the sunsets over the Bay.

But, as has been said, the whole is greater than the sum of the parts. There is a *je ne sais quoi*, an indefinable element, that makes visitors and residents alike relax, take a deep breath, and enjoy life. The folks are friendly, the atmosphere is relaxed, and amenities abound.

So, go ahead, breathe deep and step into Rockwell, USA – Fairhope, Alabama. Welcome.

The Fairhope Writers Group

The History of Fairhope

The Land –

Our "Fairhope" bluff on the Eastern Shore of Mobile Bay was questionably Spanish territory only seventy-five years before the founders of the Single Tax Colony came here in 1894. Baldwin County was created in the Mississippi Territory in 1809 and was added to the United States when Alabama became a State in 1819. Our forested woodland of virgin timber had been occupied by Native Americans, some freed and runaway Slaves, and a few courageous Anglo-Saxon settlers.

The Single Tax Colony --

Fairhope was conceived by a group in Des Moines, Iowa, who used the theories of economist and social reformer, Henry George of San Francisco, and his book, *Progress and Poverty*. Mr. George believed that land speculation was the source of most economic woes and that the solution was that no taxes should be levied other than a "single tax" on land. While the emphasis was on economics, there was also interest in community property and amenities being co-owned by everyone in the colony.

To implement the theory, the "Single Taxers," as they became known, sought a location to establish their community. Ernest B.

Gaston, newspaperman and leader of the group, began to publish the *Fairhope Courier* newspaper in Des Moines, to promote and communicate the thinking of the enthusiasts. After checking sites on the West, Midwest, and East coasts, the Alabama Gulf Coast was selected. On November 15, 1894, twenty-eight people (including nine children) gathered on the bluff on the eastern shore of Mobile Bay and announced the launch of the Single Tax Colony, *Fairhope*. They proclaimed that it had a "fair hope" of success and proceeded to build their own Utopia. The concept attracted supporters and financial backers from around the country, drawing an eclectic assemblage of industrious, creative, and free-thinking people to the colony.

The Fairhope founders were not able to create a true single tax community as defined by Henry George, but they attempted to come as close as they could. They acquired land in the name of the Fairhope Industrial Association and leased property to those who wanted to use or live on the land. Lessees received a ninety-nine-year renewable lease, but had ownership only of the improvements upon the land.

The colony became a resort community almost from the start. The founders quickly realized that the key to their survival depended upon a connection to the outside world. One of their first undertakings was the construction of the first Fairhope wharf, which allowed visitors to come by steam-powered bay boat from Mobile and relax in the small bay cottages and hotels that sprung up along the bluff top. Vacationers came to Fairhope for many of the same reasons they do today: pleasant climate, peaceful surroundings, and the impressive scenery. Artists, writers, and craftsmen found Fairhope to be an inspiring haven for their work. Even a few nudists found it appealing!

The City of Fairhope --

The City of Fairhope was established with around 500 residents in 1908, taking over municipal services from the

Fairhope Single Tax Corporation. In the 1930s, the City became the caretaker of Fairhope's greatest assets: the beachfront park, the parklands on the bluff above the beach, Henry George Park, Knoll Park and the quarter-mile-long pier—all gifts of the Single Tax Corporation, which continues to have an active presence in the city.

Today, the Single Tax Corporation owns about 4,500 acres of land in and around Fairhope. This includes the downtown area and a little less than half of the remainder of the city. The rent paid to the Single Tax Corporation by lessees includes an amount due for state, county, and local taxes, an administrative fee to operate the corporation office, and a "demonstration fee," intended to demonstrate the usefulness of the single-tax concept. Funds from the demonstration fee are used to enhance the community by supporting things such as the public parks, the public library, Thomas Hospital, and the old City Hall (now the Fairhope Museum of History).

In the Beginning --

Before the Single Taxers came, this area was wilderness. Tristan de Luna y Arellano came into the bay in 1558 and declared it the *Bahía del Espíritu Santo,* Bay of the Holy Spirit, and found Indians by the thousands living in the area. Oyster shell middens exist today in nearby estuaries as testimony to that lifestyle when canoes were the transportation of the day. French explorers came in 1699, and Pierre Le Moyne d'Iberville and his younger brother, Sieur de Bienville, established the settlement of Mobile twenty-seven miles up-river from the bay in 1702. The city was relocated in 1711 to its current site.

During the 1700s, the French discovered the clays on the Eastern Shore to be colorful and natural for making beautiful pottery. French potter Augustine Mareschal established a kiln at the juncture of the bay and Fly Creek in the 1840s that remained in operation until the early Twentieth Century. A small French military outpost was also built at (now) Montrose, to watch for any encroachment by the Spanish from Pensacola.

The British were given the Gulf Coast in the *Treaty of Paris* in 1763 and we became a part of British West Florida. In March of 1780, the Spanish came overland from Mexico and captured Mobile, including our area. British West Florida was legally ceded to Spain in the *Peace of Paris* in 1783. Spain remained in residence for the next thirty years.

To establish the southern boundary of the United States, American surveyor Andrew Ellicott surveyed and marked the 31st parallel latitude in April 1799. That left the "toes" of Alabama, Mississippi, and Louisiana, east of New Orleans, outside of the United States. That line is north of Bay Minette.

Our region flew the independent flag of *Republic of West Florida* for a short while beginning in 1810. But, before this "Kemper Rebellion" could establish a government, the United States, without buying, paying for, or conquering anything, simply declared this area a part of the United States in 1813.

American settlers began to come to this area after Andrew Jackson defeated the Creek Indians in the Battle of Horseshoe Bend (1814), and secured South Alabama Territory for safe dwelling by Americans. Even so, ownership of this part of Baldwin County was being debated between the United States and Spain from the U.S. acquisition of the Louisiana Territory in 1803 until 1813. Many residents could speak Spanish, English, or Creek. Titles to property were via British and Spanish land grants given as rewards for faithful service to their king years earlier. After statehood, almost all deeds of record were from Spanish ownership.

The Spanish military still occupied Fort Carlota in Mobile (known under the French as *Fort Conde*). So, after Andrew Jackson resolved the Creek Indian uprising, he invited the Spaniards to leave. In a negotiated agreement, the troops went to

Pensacola, leaving only a Spanish quartermaster behind for a short time to inventory material for U.S. reimbursement. This cleared the area for American settlement.

In 1820, two Dana brothers built the first settler cabins at Point Clear, three miles south of (the future) Fairhope, on the Lavalle Spanish Land Grant. Twenty-four years later, the Point Clear hotel was built and in (circa) 1849, the settlement of Battles, a half mile north, built a wharf and made the Eastern Shore a hunting and fishing destination for Mobilians. It was on the bay boat James A. Carney to Battles Wharf in 1894 that the Single Tax colonists came and camped nearby while building Fairhope.

Our Legacy --

The history of Fairhope is not just in its proximity to Forts Morgan, Gaines, Blakeley, and Spanish Fort of Civil War infamy. We are proud to note that that war was stopped twice in Mobile Bay, by long time comrades on both sides of the battle, to care for the health of colleagues on both sides. The hospitals along the shore rendered aid to both Confederate and Federal. They later shared stories and inter-married families. The first mayor of Fairhope had been a Federal military officer. Genteel Southerners sat with die-hard Yankees and enjoyed stories spawned by maturity and human-nature. Life was good!

Fairhopers are imaginative people, a bit eccentric perhaps, but genuinely creative and sharing, as we paint a legacy that goes beyond cannon fire and world geography. We watch the sunset with friends from all over, yet we see so much more than the sun going into the bay.

RMG

Fairhope at a glance:

- Located in Baldwin County, Alabama, on the Eastern Shore of Mobile Bay between Mobile and Pensacola, Florida.
- More than 220,000 arts enthusiasts attend our annual Arts and Crafts Festival in March.
- Our downtown is alive and well, with offices, boutiques, galleries, and restaurants galore.
- Fairhope was founded in 1894 as an experiment in creating a Utopian single-tax colony.
- We are one of only three places in the world that experience jubilees, a phenomenon where all manner of sea creatures come ashore seeking oxygen.
- Among well-known authors who call Fairhope home are Winston Groom, best known for *Forest Gump*; and Rick Bragg, Pulitzer Prize winning journalist. Fannie Flagg penned *Fried Green Tomatoes at the Whistle Stop Café* living in a house on Mobile Bay and has deemed Fairhope her honorary hometown.
- Population: 19,429
- Area: 14.04 square miles
- Median age: 46
- 100 females for every 86.4 males
- Median household income: $66,157
- Median family income: $93,549
- Average high temperature: 77.9 degrees
- Average low temperature: 56.7 degrees
- Precipitation: 67.87 inches of rainfall per year
- Average days of precipitation: 118
- Humid subtropical climate
- Named best small town in the South by *Southern Living Magazine* 2016

Fairhope Means Friendship

Fairhope is the Friendship City on the Bay;
the greeters are the flowers on its corners,
and trees that light and sparkle every Christmas,
and welcoming entrepreneurs on its avenues,
and travelers who happen by and stay,
and writers and artists telling their continuing
stories.

And because its pioneers dreamed of a Utopia,
their legacy is this community of dreamers.

JM

Places of Interest

The Fairhope Museum of History
Old City Hall
24 N. Section Street

The Fairhope Museum of History is an excellent place to start learning about Fairhope. The city began as a Single Tax Colony (everyone shared a portion of a single tax), and then it grew to become a city with a creative personality. As you enter the museum's *Hall of Mayors,* you will see that Fairhope is different. It was conceived in Iowa and its first mayor was a U.S. Federal military officer that was elected shortly after the Civil War. Even the building itself has a legacy.

The museum building is the first Fairhope City Hall, which was constructed in 1928. Although the Spanish occupied this part of the Gulf Coast from 1783 until 1819, the Spanish Mission stucco facade was not to commemorate our Spanish heritage; residents simply liked the architectural style. This city hall was built to consolidate the city government: the mayor's office, the city council chamber, the fire department, and police headquarters. Three jail cells were built on the first floor behind the mayor's office: two cells for men and one for women. The town didn't have much of a need for incarceration, but a town should have a jail, so it was built into the city hall. Even with that, it wasn't easy to be thrown into jail. The liberal founding spirit was rather tolerant of most misdemeanors, with the police chief merely giving the offenders a ride home and a verbal reprimand for their actions.

The first mayor to serve in the new building was M.F. Northrup. The last mayor to preside over the city council in the building was Richard Macon. When Mayor James Nix took office in 1972, the city had already moved city hall into the old First National Bank of Fairhope building on Fairhope Avenue. In 1992, the fire department moved away to its present Ingleside Avenue site. The police remained in the old building until 2002. The building then sat empty, being used as a Halloween haunted house and for storage for a few years.

The museum opened in the building in April 2008. The exhibits inside offer fun challenges for kids, including trying their skills to unlock the original old town safe that was at home there near the desk of the chief of police through the 30s and 40s. And the two remaining jail cells provide a great photo opportunity from inside the rustic bars. In the museum hallway, the Old Colonial

Inn display has an interactive computer-based display that allows guests to click on a ring in the 151-year-old pine tree to see what events occurred on that date in history. Nooks and crannies throughout the building house changing exhibits with mementos and stories of days gone by. Knowledgeable and eager docents are on standby to tell you the story of Fairhope.

The museum is open 9 a.m. to 5 p.m., Tuesday through Saturday each week, but is closed on holidays. Each Thursday at 2 p.m., a different speaker each week gives a free one-hour talk about something of historical interest from Fairhope's past. Tourists also enjoy finding that the museum has a gift shop, bathrooms, and a built-in, original fire truck!

RMG

Fairhope Colony Cemetery
Corner of Oak and Section streets

Fairhope was established by a group of colonists with an aggressive plan to change the national economics. But the physical needs of the community were not very different from any other settlement. One such need was for a cemetery. So the founders set aside four acres on the north edge of town for deceased residents. While the land was oak laden and pretty, it was on the edge of town beside a gully that prevented easy road construction northward and was not really suitable for farming. Section Street traversed Fairhope for six blocks north of Fairhope Avenue, then curved northwest to a dead-end at the gully. There lay the Colony Cemetery.

The first gravesite was used on Independence Day 1895, only seven and a half months after driving the first stake for the colony. John Hunnell drowned in the bay that morning and a holiday picnic table was disassembled and made into the first casket in the graveyard.

Fourteen of the original twenty-eight Fairhope founders are buried in the Colony Cemetery. Therein also lie the remains of Marietta Johnson, creator of the internationally renowned organic school; Marie Howland, founder of the town library; Craig Sheldon, sculptor and artist; as well as ex-mayors, doctors, and some contemporary residents of the Fairhope Single Tax Corporation (FSTC). Mr. Hunnell's body was later relocated by his family, but because of his legacy as a founder, his gravestone remains. It is also interesting that E.B. Gaston's son, Cornelius, who came to the colony at the age of ten and continued his dad's work with the FSTC until his death, is buried *not here*, but in Memory Gardens of Fairhope on Greeno Road.

The cemetery has the ornate arched walk-in entrance at the corner of Oak and Section streets and an auto entrance one block west at Oak and Church streets. An historic placard is located on the sidewalk beside the cemetery on Oak Street and a walk-in gate is there to accommodate visitors who choose to park free in the civic center parking lot.

The cemetery continues to "accept" residents, even though requisites for who can be buried there are set by the FSTC. The grounds will accommodate approximately 2,500 gravesites. The requirements have the unique provision that vaults or caskets must be at least fourteen inches below the surface, and a spouse is buried on top of his/her predeceased partner, to save space. The care and maintenance of individual graves and monuments are the responsibility of family and friends. The general care and maintenance of the cemetery is partly funded with donations to the FSTC for that purpose.

RMG

A Moment of Necessity

Yes, it happens to all of us sooner or later. We need a rest stop. No matter how hard you beg, the shops in Fairhope have no public access to rest rooms. Take heart though, this writer has scouted out even the most obscure of places to take care of this matter.

The primary public restroom in the shopping area is located at the Welcome Center on Section Street. Right next door is the Fairhope Museum of History, which also has public restrooms. Other restrooms are located in the entrance to the French Quarter, across from the Panini Pete's dining room.

If the urge strikes on the Church Street side of downtown, there are public facilities in a corner of the Community Park. You can enter the park on Church Street or from Morphy Avenue.

You may be strolling along the bayfront when you need a stop, and restrooms are located in the beach area or mid-way on the Fairhope Pier. Up on the bluff, you can visit the facility at the Pier Street boat launch.

As you can *see*, there is a solution for every urgent problem. Happy resting!

RG

The Fairhope Pier

We all remember the Three Stooges putdown, "Hey, buddy, why don't you take a long walk on a short pier." But since Fairhope has a long pier, we recommend you just take a long walk—at least to the end of it.

First, before you take your long walk, we also recommend you visit our rose garden and fountain in the traffic circle. We would like to direct your attention to the size of the roses and, equally important, the size of the trunks of the rose plants. Yes, some of

those roses are older than your uncle's favorite pair of shoes hidden way in the back of his closet. This is why the rosebuds are so large and wonderful. But you are not here only to see the roses; you are here to take that famous long walk on a long pier.

We would love to say this pier was built in 1876, before there was a Fairhope and about the time the town was named "Alabama City," but one or two of the local historians would come out of the woodwork. Truth is, there are lots of official maps with the name "Alabama City" squarely on top of where Fairhope stands today.

But enough about that, back to the pier. There are hundreds of pictures scattered all over town of the pier in its younger days. It has been rebuilt several times, due to the hurricanes that come and smash things up. Even before the Civil War, steam-powered bay boats ferried passengers over here from Mobile. Children would use the thirty-foot water slide to slip headlong into the warm waters of the bay. Fishermen would stand for hours catching "tonight's meal" out of the bay.

Today, alas, there are no steam-driven bay boats, but children still swim off the beaches to the north. The only things that have remained the same are the fishermen and the fish. If you see something silvery jump out of the water and disappear quickly, those are mullet. We expect they are only teasing the fishermen. "Betcha can't catch me." Yes, there are many pole fishermen, but if you have good timing, you may catch several fishing aficionados casting nets into the grey green waters of the bay. While it is not high art, this comes close to tossing a perfect Frisbee. The art is all about how you hold the cast net and how to fling it. You'll want it to hit the water in the largest circle possible, then sink quickly to entangle a couple of jumping mullet unaware of what is about to happen to them. If you haven't brought a fishing rod or a cast net, and have a taste for fish, look over there, why there is a sea food restaurant right there.

The Pier Bar and Grill is run by the Gambino family, which has been plying their trade in the restaurant business for three generations. Menu items run from po' boys to shrimp, crab, oysters, catfish, and chicken—plus good appetizers. Not to mention, the bay view is the best in town. One last thing we might mention is this, if you are thinking of walking off the pier for a quick swim, don't. The waters here are not that deep. Maybe five to six feet at the most. So, if someone says, "Hey, buddy, why don't you take a long walk off a short pier," my advice is jump right in. You can always walk back to the shore, maybe with a mullet in your pocket.

How to get there? Stand anywhere on Fairhope Avenue and start walking west toward the bay. When your feet are wet, stop. You are in the fountain and the pier is right there in front of you. A must.

RM

Marietta Johnson Museum

10 South School Street

The Marietta Johnson Museum is located in the rear of the Bell Building on the campus of Coastal Alabama Community College. Here you will learn about one of the earliest and most successful progressive-enlightenment schools in the United States and, indeed, in the world, The School of Organic Education. Cynthia "Maggie" Mosteller-Timbes, the museum director, will guide you and explain the many exhibits of interesting artifacts, photographs, documents, and letters pertaining to this unique school. A short film presentation is available.

Mrs. Johnson was invited to come to Fairhope in 1907 to establish a free school for Fairhope's children. She accepted and founded her "organic school" that same year, putting into practice her educational philosophy and those of the most progressive educational theorists of the time, such as John Dewey, the father of progressive education, and Nathan Oppenheim.

There were no tests, no grades. However, this was not a "do as you please, goof off" school. Students were encouraged to do their best, develop character, and love learning. There were no failures at the organic school, since children advanced at their own pace. They were given multiple opportunities to learn by doing. Mrs. Johnson believed that "all learning is through experience." Dewey, who visited and endorsed the school, commented, "Here, the technique is good and the children are free."

Mrs. Johnson operated the school until her death in 1938. It remains open, taught by her successors following her philosophy. Over the years, the school has gone in and out of favor, but has continuously kept it doors open for 112 years. Formerly including Pre-K through 12th grade, the school currently focuses on young students from Pre-K through 2nd Life (3rd and 4th grade). Many of the students have gone on to attend universities and enjoyed successful careers.

The museum is free and is open to the public from Monday through Saturday by appointment. Group tours are also available. For appointments, please email Maggie or Wayne at mariettajohnson@mindspring.com. For more information, please visit the museum's website at http://www.mariettajohnson.org.

JW

Magnolia Beach on the Bay Front
South Mobile Street

What better place is there on the Eastern Shore to watch the sunset than Magnolia Beach? There isn't one! Twenty-three park benches facing west overlooking Mobile Bay for almost a quarter mile, are waiting for you and your pet. The low bluff allows a clear view of the evening sun, as mullet jump and occasionally dolphins lazily surface in the still water. Dogs walk their owners, as they (the dogs) sniff along and stop at pet water fountains along the way. The concrete walkway winds casually through oaks bearing Spanish moss and azaleas blooming in the spring. The robust benches are there for tired strollers and the city-sponsored bronze artwork reminds us of our artistic past. The view is also appealing to bikers, likers, and hikers who want to be outdoors for the salty breeze and exercise. The bay to the west and historic homes on the east take you back in time.

The park is on Mobile Street along the bayfront between Pier and Laurel Avenues. Or, more easily spotted on the north end is the boat launch at Pier Avenue and on the south, the American Legion Lodge where the street curves away from the shore to avoid banging into the side of the historic ladies hotel, turned patriotic lodge.

Magnolia Beach is the older of Fairhope's two shoreline parks, but the newer of the community owned parks. It's the one farther south beginning at Pier Street and ending at the American Legion Lodge. Parking is convenient (ten spaces) at the short pier across from Orange Avenue near Trinity Presbyterian Church, and on the north end of the park at the boat launch area. Restrooms are also at the launch. The Orange Avenue pier reaches into the bay to accommodate fishermen seeking a couple of hours of aquatic therapy or to cast a net to see what's there.

For boaters, the Pier Avenue launch area is free to put your boat into the bay and to park vehicle and trailer, but launching there can be treacherous if the wind is blowing. The beautiful waters of the bay are shallow and can whip up white-capped waves quickly, making getting into boats and boat rides perilous. The nostalgic barnacled old pier posts off shore are picturesque, but can create underwater obstacles for novice mariners trying out new boats.

The unseen story of this park is its history. In the 1920s, this south shore area became lined with beachfront cottages and was used for bathhouses and boardwalks. The residents legally named the stretch Magnolia Beach and combined their deeds into a public park. During the depression years of the 1930s, the property owners fell into arrears on their taxes and the City of Fairhope bought the property in 1934. Litigation came about in the 1960s, when a civic club wanted to buy Magnolia Park for its own use and "straighten Mobile Street." The City of Fairhope decided it didn't need the park and agreed to sell it. But an uproar of public opinion brought on the contest and after months of debate, in January 1965, the Alabama Supreme Court ruled the sale unconstitutional. It had been originally deeded with the caveat that it remain a park. Today, it's still a park and there's still a curve in Mobile Street.

RMG

Fairhope Public Library

501 Fairhope Avenue

Perhaps it seems odd to include something as commonplace as a public library in our walking tour, but our library is, most assuredly, not commonplace. It is an excellent source of learning, with an outstanding collection in an architecturally distinguished building at the corner of Bancroft Street and Fairhope Avenue. Fairhope has bragging rights for having the first public library in the state of Alabama.

Our library's vision statement is a reflection of the cultural needs and desires of our diverse citizenry. Founded in 1900 with the personal collection of early resident Marie Howland, it currently serves, in keeping with that vision statement, "as a guide to world-wide information, a center for learning activity and a source for leisure materials."

It is a rare day in Fairhope when there is not an interesting program to attend for both adults and children at our library. The Consanguinity movie program runs all summer, with a free movie, cookies, lemonade, and tea. There are book review programs, a non-fiction book club, computer classes, Monday movies for children, and story time for ages two and under. We have an exceptional genealogy club to help discover family roots. Computer carrels are open and available for residents' use. Books, audio books, reference materials, CDs, and DVDs are all available.

The Friends of the Fairhope Library run a used book shop in the southeast corner featuring bargains on books, as well as CDs, DVDs, magazines, and audio books. Addicted bibliophiles can feed their addiction at book sales held throughout the year where prices are reduced even further.

Check out the library's web site calendar to see what is listed to spend a quiet, cool, and educational interlude.

RG

American Legion
700 S. Mobile Street

Standing in queenly splendor, this three-story, white frame building stands on a bluff overlooking Mobile Bay. She has stood at this location since 1912, withstanding dozens of tropical storms and hurricanes. This is the current location of American Legion Post 199. The top two floors of the building are used for storage right now, but the main floor holds a friendly bar, open to the public, and a recently renovated hall with a kitchen and stage available for parties, weddings, and corporate events. The beachfront, with an outdoor stage and Tiki Bar, is also available for private parties.

In the days before unchaperoned ladies could casually check into a hotel, the building was intended as an accommodation for ladies visiting Fairhope from across the bay or across the country. Built by a benevolent organization that helped women trying to get into business, the group was defunct by the late 1920s. It then became the Women's Yacht Club, in conjunction with the Eastern Shore Yacht Club, whose clubhouse stood across the street. Socials and dances were held there. Beginning in the late 1930s, the building became a boarding house, housing families and singles, particularly after the Mobile population tripled during

World War II. The American Legion organization bought the structure at the end of the war and installed a boxing ring on the third floor, where pugilistic bouts were held.

In the early 1960s, the building was enlarged by enclosing the sleeping porches circling the perimeter. This gracious grand dame lost her National Historic Register status when the porches were enclosed, but she is a Fairhope treasure none the less.

Today, from the porch on the back of the building, customers can sit and watch the spectacular sunsets on the bay. The Legion hosts public barbeques on Memorial Day, Fourth of July, Labor Day, and Veterans Day, where members and visitors alike can enjoy barbequed chicken and pulled pork dinners. There are frequent summer concerts on the Legion beachfront, with drinks available at the Tiki Bar. *Monday Night Mess Hall* dinners are held every Monday beginning at 5 p.m., where a home-cooked meal is available, prepared by the ladies of the Legion Auxiliary. Other nights, patrons may find spaghetti or tacos served at the bar while they watch news or sports on the big-screen TVs.

The American Legion is a veterans' organization worth supporting. The building is historic, the beach view is gorgeous, and the drinks are affordable. Stop by Post 199 for a cold drink, support the Vets, and get a taste of history.

RG

Markers of Sorts

I was asked recently, "If Fairhope is historic, where are the historic homes, gun emplacements, and monuments?" Well, ...we're not *that kind* of historic town! There were no battles fought here, nor are there monuments "bearing arms." The antebellum homes are over in Mobile and plantations are somewhere upstate. So then, why are there 111 historic "shields and banners" displayed on cottages, beach houses, and landmarked buildings, promoting the appeal of Fairhope since the late 1800s? I guess we're just proud of our Utopia!

As you walk, you will find granite monuments honoring veterans and citing the virtues of Fairhope Single Tax founder, Henry George. (George never came to Fairhope, by the way. It was, however, his economic philosophy that spawned the colony.)

The oldest home marked with a shield is Dr. Mershon's home, built in 1897 near the heart of town in the 200 block of Fairhope Avenue. A homestead a little further south, in the 19000 block of Scenic Highway 98/Mobile Street, was built in 1841. As you peruse Fairhope's streets and alleyways, you will find homes of settlers marked with a colorful Baldwin County emblem and a ribbon beneath, denoting the heritage of the home and year it was built. Among these buildings sporting markers are four churches, one now housing Theatre 98 at Morphy Avenue and Church Street.

There are several traditional historical markers around town too. Some are placed by the City of Fairhope near the pier and rose garden at the bay, and up on the bluff. The Colony Cemetery has one, and the first Christian church in Fairhope is marked at the corner of Fairwood Boulevard and Patlynn Drive, even though it has moved from its original location. The Friends of the Museum of History also recently unveiled a marker on the Coastal Alabama College campus noting the home sites of Nancy Lewis, ex-Slave who sold land to the colony founders, and Stewart the Picture Man, who caught the development of Fairhope on film, or glass plates as it was, for thirty-five years.

Of equal enjoyment are the bronze statues downtown at the Welcome Center, at Thomas Hospital, and along Mobile Street at the bay. A five-foot Marietta Johnson sits on the flowered bluff above the city pier and reads to students, as matriarch of the organic school that began in Fairhope in 1907. And on a brief walk south, you find Magnolia Beach Park, which has other artistic statues, including an impressive dolphin  dancing on its tail as you stroll the pathway.

If you're really an eccentric about this sort of thing, you can find a private seven-foot obelisk in the back yard of a home at Ingleside and Estella Streets in memory of a gentleman's horse. A wealthy businessman from Birmingham moved to Fairhope and brought his horse. When he (the horse) died, he got a monument. Remember this is on private property.

On a smaller scale, as you walk around downtown, you will see personalized paver stones. About a decade ago, the city was short on funds and needed to repave the sidewalks. As a fundraiser, the people of Fairhope bought a paver and put their name, family member, or a memory on it, and the city curbed the stones along Fairhope Avenue. You can also find similar stones at Theatre 98 and in the courtyard of the Fairhope Museum of History. It's a way to leave your own monument in Fairhope. Or you can join the Single Tax Corporation and put your own stake in the ground with a ninety-nine-year lease.

RMG

Lagniappe

And Parking is Always Free

Most of our visitors remark about the *laissez faire* parking system we enjoy here in Fairhope. In other words, you park anywhere you like and there will be no parking meters and no *"2 Hour Parking-- Strictly Enforced"* signs. Nope, not here. You can park your car downtown in front of "Elwood's House of Easily Repairable Furniture" and leave it there for three days, and, sure enough, when you return from wherever you have been hiding or shopping or sleeping, your car will still be there and with no white ticket flapping on your windshield wiper.

We like visitors and want them to enjoy their time here. It's like visiting relatives. They would not think to charge you money for parking in their driveway during your visit, and neither do we.

But if you happen to find yourself in Fairhope when everybody and his brother are in town for some event, like the *"Prettiest Mother-in-Law Contest,"* then here are a few dedicated places you can park your car—and park for free. First is the city parking lot across the street from the Fairhope Public Library on Bancroft and Fairhope Avenue near Julwin's Restaurant. Number two is the big cement three-story parking structure behind the "Little Whiskey Christmas Club," which is on Church Street. Your advantage there is that much of the parking is covered, so if you're driving a car and the back window won't roll up and you know it's going to rain, then this is the place for you. The third secret place is off Church Street behind the Fairhope Inn. There is a secret short cut walk through the French Quarter. Stop and enjoy the best hamburger in town at *Panini Pete's gastronomic establishment.* The fourth parking lot, and it is a bit further away, is the one near our civic center and Colony Cemetery just across from the Art Center. There are some shade trees there.

One last thought—and it is a piece of wisdom from my good friend Nevin Voglesong, who stars in a movie called *The Ruby Glasses,* which is free on YouTube. He maintains small towns across America lost their devotees when shopping centers offered unlimited free parking and little downtowns still had parking meters with one-hour parking, and unsmiling police who willy-nilly wrote parking tickets. Nevin says people rushed to the shopping centers because of the huge free parking lots. Fairhopians never rushed to those shopping center parking lots because there is something in us that was inherited from our forefathers that instinctively values a small downtown with plenty of parking and lots of little independent stores selling one-of-a-kind things, or restaurants which may surprise you with their delectable offerings. And that, dear reader, is just one reason why Fairhope is what it is today. Some call it Pleasantville by the Bay. We call it home. Enjoy it. And enjoy our free parking.

RM

Bits, Bites, & Beverages

The Book Cellar
32 South Section (Entrance off De la Mare)

This is one of the newest full bars in Fairhope and has the distinction of residing in the rear of a famous bookstore/coffee shop. Sometimes it's like having a beer and burger in Grand Central Station while watching commuters rush by.

Meanwhile, this intimate bar is becoming the hangout of some of the region's best bands and best single performers. Every Monday night the place is packed starting at 5 p.m. and going to 7 p.m. with a talented singer/song writer. Sometimes it's a group of five that crowds the stage. Keifer Wilson runs the place, and his big smile and friendliness ensure a good time is had by all. Friday night finds the place packed out again, and the music can last until it's time to roll up the sidewalks.

One of the bartenders is Molly Thomas, who might grab her violin and take center stage. A week later, Molly might open for a big name rock star a thousand miles away. But for now, she is ours and the Book Cellar is her home when she is not touring. Check their web site for who is playing. A must.

RM

Fairhope Chocolate
French Quarter

My good friend, Adora Nuberberger, claims that chocolate keeps her alive. She also claims it saved her marriage. And if that is even slightly true, she lives in the right place to indulge in the best chocolate in seventeen states.

I am not saying thousands of chocoholics make pilgrimages to Fairhope for the indescribable, on your tongue heaven in a bite. But then, a lot of them do.

So, why is this quaint little chocolate shoppe located in Fairhope and how did it get started? Some say Jule Roach, who is the wizard behind the curtain, and her husband, Dr. Roach, traveled to Belgium a while back, and while walking around Bruges, happened to wander into a chocolate shop and there tasted Neuhaus Chocolate. Kaboom! Magic happened. Bells went off, and a thought popped into Jule's brain. She said, "Why can't we get this chocolate in the United States?" From that point on, Jule was on a mission. And the mission had two parts. One was to import and sell Neuhaus Chocolate, and two was to learn how to make her own brand of chocolate, which she now calls Fairhope Chocolate.

This brings us to the delicious parts of this story. One of the many creations Adora Nuberberger loves is the chocolate turtles. The caramel is made to a secret old world formula that only Jule knows, and the plump pecans are handpicked at B & B Pecans here in Fairhope. Ursula (not her real name), who works for Jule and knows almost as much about being a chocolatier chef, said Adora also adores the dark chocolate bark with macadamia nuts and cranberries. I tasted the coconut and almond 64 percent dark chocolate bark, and instantly fell in love with Ursula. Ursula says men fall in love with her all the time after tasting their chocolate. She says university research proves chocolate triggers the love neuron. I agree.

Jule says they offer classes in making chocolate, and one of their specialties is not chocolate at all, but a caramel apple. So if you are looking for a treat after a great lunch, we suggest stopping in. It began in the French Quarter right across from Panini Pete's, but will be moving to Fairhope Avenue near Honeybaked Ham. It's a little pricey, but that's the cost of falling in love.

RM

Latté Da (in Page & Palette)
32 South Section Street

Our good friend, Nesgood Truman, says if he were president of the United States, he would mandate that every town have a coffee shop exactly like the Latté Da, and every Latté Da coffee shop have a book store attached exactly like the Page and Palette. This, by the way, is located almost in the center of town, at Section and De la Mare streets.

Nesgood says he meets the most interesting people there every day. He says senators, baseball players, Hollywood actors, fired college professors, artists, old leftists, young pretty mothers, and about everybody else you would like to meet come there to chat over a morning coffee or espresso. Then in the afternoon, people chat over a scoop of ice cream, a glass of sweet tea, or the best carrot cake in three states. Five of the prettiest girls vie for the barista of the day. They will give you a big Southern smile, and one is filled with information she might share—or not, depending on whether you can keep a secret.

And if you are looking for some therapy, wait around till before noon and two of our town's wisest ladies, Nancy and Sonya, will open their free advice booth over in the corner and chat with you for five minutes or half an hour depending on your schedule. Yes, they say it is free, but in the end they charge five cents for their time and their considerable and above average wisdom. These delightful girls say they got the idea from Lucy's booth in the Peanuts comic strip. Nesgood sits at their booth on a child's stool, and he is especially taken with Nancy's advice, although Sonya is a quick witted one who gets in her two cents whenever she can.

Now if you're into the "internest"—that's what Nesgood calls it—Latté Da does have free Wi-Fi, although the political conversations over in the corner are way better than anything you can find on television or the internest. You may notice that Keifer, who is the co-owner, also has good advice; he is the one who is more dressed up than most of us and is constantly adjusting the chairs, straightening the place, and holding the door open for the moms who come with their strollers. Nesgood says the prettiest moms with the prettiest babies stroll in every fifteen minutes or so, to meet another pretty mom with a baby cuter than the one before.

Latté Da is also famous for its sidewalk table and chairs, where you can enjoy your coffee, smoothie, or tea.

You may think I have forgotten the bookstore, which is in the same building. No, I haven't. Nesgood says he has never met a group of more charming, knowledgeable book ladies. He calls them bookristas. They must read a book a night to keep up with what is the latest and greatest. Plus there is a special section where everybody who works in the store displays their favorite books of the month. My book was once a favorite of three of the girls, and that was the highlight for the whole year for me. I will not tell you the names of my books, as this is not the point of this review, and further, Nesgood would look down on me for doing that. If you're staying here for a day or so, you should ask one of the bookristas when the next book signing is happening. We have had all the big names and most of the *New York Times* best-sellers over the years. Fannie Flagg, who wrote *Fried Green Tomatoes*, stops by now and then to chat with Karin, who now runs the place with her husband, Keifer.

Another big name writer you have probably heard about—and one who Nesgood says is the best history writer next to David McCullough—is Winston Groom. Sure everybody knows about his first novel, *Forrest Gump*, but just open one of his books on any history subject, and you are sucked in till the end. Winston stops in all the time, and if he is not here, he is three miles down the road at Point Clear, where he has surrounded himself with thirty stacks of notes and is working on his next book.

We also have some local writers who sit around outside just listening to conversations and taking notes, probably to appear as conversation in their next books. I myself have done that. Oh yes, one last thing. If you see what you think are a couple of down and out bums sitting outside or in, do not be misled. One is a former editor of the *New York Times*, and the other is a Pulitzer Prize winning writer. We even have a couple of retired actors who used to live in Hollywood and you might recognize them. Then, too, you might not. And that's okay with them.

RM

Mr. Gene's Beans
310 De la Mare

For such a small store, Mr. Gene's Beans on De la Mare will be a wonderful surprise when you discover the more than huge selection of refreshments inside. Let us start with the coffee. On the wall you will see six chalkboards listing all the different coffees they can make for the discerning customer. My wife had an ever popular latté, and said it was quite good. I had a café Americano and it was on the mark. There are two baristas behind the counter, so there should not be much of a wait. Unlike Starbucks, with its rubber stamp atmosphere and its cold efficiency, Gene's Beans tries for small town personality. The girls are friendly and quick. They wear no uniforms, and you might recognize one from the marching band at last Friday night's Fairhope High School football game.

You can sit inside and enjoy your cup or, if so inclined, you may find a seat outside on the raised deck overlooking De la Mare. We sat at a table with an umbrella overhead and watched the sidewalk amblers stroll by. And while it is not the same as sitting at a sidewalk café in Paris, it produces the same lost-in-time relaxation vibe we so love about sidewalk cafés.

Now to the icing on the cake. Chris and Chad Bartz have the largest selection of ice cream in Fairhope. I counted twenty-four varieties, from the ever popular vanilla to rocky road, cookies and crumbs, peach delight, rainbow, purple rain, cherries jubilee, bubble gum, and the list goes on and on. The best part is, they change the flavors about once a week, so there is always something new to taste. This fun shop exclusively scoops Blue Bell ice cream, which most would say is the best ice cream around. And for my wife, his frozen yogurt is always her penultimate. Got thirty minutes to kill? We know just the right place to rest your tootsies. *RM*

Red or White Wine and Gourmet Center
323A De la Mare Avenue

If you are looking for somewhere to buy a bottle of wine or perhaps to enjoy a glass of wine or two in a pleasant, inviting setting, the Red or White Wine and Gourmet Center is a superb choice. Red or White, locally owned by Randy and Sherri Williams, is both a wine store and a wine bar. At any given time, you will have 500 or so red and white wine selections available to satisfy every taste and budget. You can complement your choice of wine with choices of Bruschetta, cheese and meat boards, small plates, and ten-inch thin crust "award winning pizzas."

The friendly and knowledgeable staff is always ready to assist you in wine and food pairing selections. This writer's favorite is a red cabernet sauvignon paired with their Sampler Board offering two meats, one cheese, beans, olives, and two Bruschetta pieces. His choice of small plates is the Italian Sausage simmered in red wine and rosemary, and finished with shaved parmesan. The board and plate presentations are all tempting, and the wonderful aromas of pizza preparations will entice you toward a pizza choice. This writer is confident you will enjoy the casual atmosphere and be well satisfied whichever wine and food pairing you may make. It is all great. Enjoy!

JW

Refuge Coffee
4 South Bancroft

As you may have noticed, there is no ubiquitous Starbuck's coffee shop in Fairhope. Nor is there San Francisco's famous Café Trieste here, but rest assured your desire for an excellent rich coffee can be quenched in our little village; Refuge Coffee Shop will fit the bill nicely. It is a far cry from the cluttered and mismatched chaired store front, folk-singing coffee shops of the seventies, and certainly not decorated with the semi-hip organic earth colors of Starbucks or Seattle's Best or Peets. No, this décor is new industrial steel, raw wood with white painted walls bearing only spartan decorations of a few simple black and white photos, all equally spaced and hanging on thin silver threads.

But décor is not why you come here. No, you come for the coffee. And what delicious coffees they have. The baristas are hip guys who can tell you the proper temperature at which coffee should be brewed (198-204 degrees), and they wear the hats of aficionados. They might ask you a few questions before making a recommendation. And since the owner, the tall guy with the beard, recently operated a coffee shop somewhere in Central America, he can tell you what the beans will taste like once roasted properly. My favorite is the Café Americano. Two shots of rich robust espresso, add some hot water and steamed milk and *voila*, you and your morning coffee are bonded and off to a great start.

They also have a test tube row of what appears to be a chemistry experiment in which they make the best slow-drip coffee you have tasted. A friend commented that the whole place looks like a coffee experiment laboratory sometime in the near future. And maybe that's why the coffee is so darn good. They know exactly what they are doing. They also have pastry. A must.

RM

Soul Bowlz

68 N. Bancroft Street

If you are looking for something cool and refreshing, or a healthy breakfast or snack, or a bit of a rest in an interesting, relaxing environment, Soul Bowlz answers on all counts.

With names like Mind, Body, Karma, Soul, and Ocean, these handcrafted superfruit-based creations have got to be good for, well, mind, body, and soul.

Open 9-5 Monday through Saturday and 11-5 Sunday, Soul Bowlz has become a regular for many Fairhope residents and is a cool find for visitors. Soul Bowlz calls their fruit bowls "a nutrient packed bowl of wholesome goodness with blend choices of acai, pitaya, graviola, and acerola." These superfruits are harvested from the amazon of South America and are both nutritious and energy enhancing. All bowls are topped with granola, fresh fruits, and honey. If you choose, you can add toppings such as cacao nibs, Nutella, peanut butter, bee pollen, and much more.

Their smoothies use no ice, so you are getting full fruit and nutrients. Now there is value. There is something for everyone! Even the kids come in clamoring for a green smoothie, not knowing they are enjoying spinach and kale in their blended fruity treat.

Just look for the purple building across from the Mill and get ready for an awesome treat, good for the body, good for the soul.

PP

Tongue and Groove Drinkery
77 S Section Street

One of Fairhope's newest additions to establishments for libation, Tongue and Groove touts themselves as a proper drinkery for stylish people to relax. While they don't actually take themselves too seriously, they are serious about serving quality hand crafted cocktails. They make their own syrups and take pride in creativity.

Folks who've been there agree that Tongue and Groove is sleek and chic, but also a lot of fun.

PP

The Yard Milkshake Bar

108 N. Section Street

Chelsea Green wanted to open an ice cream shop "like no other dessert place she had ever been to." With The Yard, she succeeded in spades, with specialty milkshakes like nothing you've ever seen in an ice cream  shop. While they do offer regular milkshakes, cones, and bowls, their specialty milkshakes are like edible art, or maybe even architecture. But be sure you are either really hungry or sharing.

Take, for instance, the Peanut Butter Brownie Bliss. Start with a pint jar that's had the rim dipped in peanut butter and is then filled with brownie batter ice cream and chocolate chips. On top of that put whipped cream, peanut butter cups, fudge, and peanut butter drizzle. As if that isn't already over the top, add a whole fudge brownie. See? Edible architecture. An ice cream sky scraper.

If you are celebrating a birthday while you're in town, The Yard will host your birthday party. Or just come in to see if you can really eat a whole Unicorn.

PP

Living High on the Hog at the Pig

Driving into Fairhope, a billboard proclaims the location of the largest wine selection in Baldwin County. I enjoy a glass of wine with dinner, or just to relax in the evening. Or with a special lunch. Or to celebrate a special occasion. Or to liven up the Cheerios at breakfast. Just kidding. I don't know how to wine pair with Cheerios. It's hard enough with shredded wheat.

At any rate, I certainly wanted to visit the wine store, so I drove over to 100 Plantation Pointe at the intersection of Greeno Road and Fairhope Avenue. I was dubious when I arrived. It did not look like I expected, yet it was familiar. Inside, I saw so much more than wine. There was a wide variety of gourmet treats. Lartigue's, a seafood store, was snugged into one corner, with fresh from the sea offerings and already cooked seafood dishes. (You may be staying in a rental cottage with a full kitchen, but there should really be no pressure to actually cook while you're on vacation.)

I smelled major deliciousness and followed my nose to a sign that said Andree's. I very quickly discovered that Andree's has been a household name in Fairhope for more than thirty years and is synonymous with scrumptious foods and quality catering. They were a deli, bakery, and restaurant downtown for most of those years and are now located within the same walls as this fine wine purveyor.

My hubby even found a humidor with choice cigars at the end of a wine aisle. Would the wonders never end?

The biggest surprise of all, however, should be that many of the employees in this culinary gold mine wear shirts proclaiming, "We Dig the Pig," complete with a big picture of that creature.

Yes, folks, all this goodness was located in the Fairhope Piggly Wiggly grocery store. I remember the Piggly Wiggly near my grandparents' house in Collins, Miss., and, believe me, it was nothing like the one I was standing in. This ain't your mama's Piggly Wiggly.

PP

The old Fairhope Post office on Fairhope Avenue (pictured left in 1932) was transformed into the offices of the Fairhope Courier, *and is now the site of Merchants and Marine Bank (right). Whatever its incarnation, the building draws attention for its architecture. Some elements of the original structure have been preserved by the bank.*

Photos courtesy of M&M Bank.

Alley Bistro and Wine Bar

312 Fairhope Avenue

Besides being a wonderful setting, this venue, which takes up most of the Mediterranean-style alleyway, is a prize we cherish. Outside and inside dining is always a treat, but what is on the menu makes it a find. Ashley and Wade have done a splendid job in creating a menu that is one of the most inventive around. Yes, it has a Mediterranean flair, but toss in some French touches and you have a fine dining experience.

I will start with the appetizer menu. Bruschetta and Caprese spring rolls and stuffed mushroom du jour make it difficult to decide. Then come a long list of salads, each one a delight. From there, we sampled the sandwiches and could not have been happier. The bread is a standout, as it is homemade on premises each morning, and comes with a crunch and texture found usually in Italy. Ashley tries to buy as much locally grown produce and cheese and meats as are available. This may account for the riches of flavors you will experience.

For dinner, Chef Wade's roots shine through. We especially loved the lamb, but fresh seafood ran a close second, and the Chicken Marsala was a standout. Glorious pasta with a delectable selection of sauces follows closely. And just a little way up the alley is the Alley Wine Bar, which is also a part of this conspiracy. Food from the Alley Bistro is served here also. As a matter of fact, watch out for waiters running up and down the alley carrying hot plates to diners at the wine bar.

The Bistro is open seven days a week 11 to 3 and then reopens at 5 until 9 for evening dining. On the weekends they stay open until 10. This is a welcomed addition to our town's restaurants, especially for those craving a new dining experience several notches above the expected. Prices are reasonable. A must.

RM

Another Broken Egg Café
300 Fairhope Avenue

This breakfast and lunch café is a place where you can order a bloody Mary with your early morning omelet should you want. It is located in an appealing exterior natural brick and wood building with a pleasing interior of mauve painted walls and natural brick. Local art work and a large clock, visible from everywhere inside, adorn the walls.

Another Broken Egg is open every day of the week from 7:00 a.m., until 2:00 p.m. You may sit at a table, a booth, or on a bar stool. And, in fact, an untold number of eggs are broken each day to accommodate the varied and tempting menu.

Their menu includes crab cake, brisket, and smoked salmon benedicts; a lobster & brie omelet, and, this writer's favorite, a seared sea scallop omelet, and many other egg dishes, plus pancakes, waffles, and French toast. And, by the way, an array of different bloody Mary mixes and mimosa cocktails are available by the glass or pitcher. Spiked cold coffee brews are also offered.

A friendly wait staff is ready to serve you. This is an interesting, pleasing café to enjoy either breakfast or lunch or both.

JW

Bay Breeze Café
50 S. Church Street

The casual, airy interior of the café is inviting, but outside, umbrella-shielded tables allow you to people watch as you eat. Bay Breeze offers an interesting and varied menu. Lunch is offered from 11-2:30 Monday through Saturday and breakfast is served on Friday and Saturday from 8-10:30.

The lunch menu includes a variety of soups, salads, wraps, sandwiches, specialty dogs, and pita pizzas. The shrimp and Conecuh on a grilled hoagie with peppers, onions, and boom boom sauce piqued my interest, but there are plenty more delicious creations to choose from.

Breakfast offerings include Gouda grit cakes; bacon, egg, and cheese quesadillas; English muffins; and more. The coffee is fresh, hot, and perfectly brewed.

On a recent breakfast visit, a thin woman in a bright pink silky shirt at the next table leaned toward me. "You should come back at lunch," she said. "They are practically famous for their tomato bisque. And their desserts?" She kissed her fingertips. "To die for."

"My mom makes them," commented the woman who had taken my order, as she placed my food on the table. "I'm Julie Tew," said the server. "This is my place."

The silky pink lady cried, "How wonderful," and began asking questions about the restaurant and the owner. I ate my breakfast, which was as good as it had sounded, and learned about the history of the place by way of the conversation beside me. Julie had opened it in 2004 in order to stay in her native Fairhope to be near her parents. Having worked in various restaurants since her early 20s, she decided to open her own and stay put. It has been a hit, and the menu is updated every year after the annual spring art show, which is a big draw in Fairhope.

Having learned that the featured dessert was a secret-recipe Southern Pecan Delight, made with pecans grown on the family's own forty acres, I ordered the blonde brownie-type confection to take home for afternoon coffee and made a mental note to meet friends for lunch at Bay Breeze.

PP

Bone and Barrel
311 Fairhope Avenue

Bone and Barrel is located in a two-story building that offers three places to dine: downstairs, the patio, and upstairs with a view of downtown Fairhope.

B&B is known for their three-napkin, really large sandwiches, which usually cover the plate. When they hit a homerun it is outstanding, but sometimes they miss. The Debris Po'boy is known far and wide as unique and quite flavorful. We give it four stars. Again, there is plenty to eat. The rooster sandwich is an overdressed chicken sandwich held together with a steak knife.

Interesting curb appeal, but in the end it is average. The seared tuna gets great marks, as does the Triple B Burger. We are not crazy about the ribs, in that there is nothing special about them. Also the salads could be more imaginative. We are, however, totally crazy about their grilled shrimp appetizer, and their fries are par excellence.

The patio, where smokers are welcome, features live loud get-up-and-dance music on the weekends. Open daily 11 a.m. to 10 p.m., their service is uneven. Great atmosphere, though it can be a little noisy. Good selection of beer. I recommend you come very hungry, as you will not leave disappointed.

RM

Cactus Cantina
108 North Section Street

This Tex-Mex chain restaurant has possibly one of the nicest locations in town. You can sit outside under large umbrellas in the courtyard and enjoy the surroundings and your meal. That said, the food is not getting great marks from many, and it appears the reasoning is that the dishes do not have the spice and flavors one comes to expect from an authentic Mexican restaurant. However, many customers like it for that very reason. Some are new to town and want a predictable bland Mexican meal with no surprises, and while you won't get a bad meal here, you won't get a great one either. Service can be slow and they do not always get your order right. If you are in a large party and want to sit in a terrific setting, this could be the spot for you.

RM

Camellia Café
61 N. Section Street

This is the perfect dinner place for special occasions such as a romantic evening with your loved one. Here is where you will find white tablecloths, delicately folded white napkins, a red rose, and wine glasses waiting atop your table. And, it is where friendly and helpful staff will greet and serve you.

A worldwide wine list and a dinner menu offering salads; entrees including grilled filet of beef, roasted duck breast, and a variety of locally acquired seafood; and vegetables and fruits, all elegantly prepared by Chef Ryan, are yours to choose. This writer's choice from the gourmet desert menu is the bourbon pecan pie with ice-cream, but there are other choices just as delicious.

Cocktails prepared by a mixologist from the full bar of assorted quality whiskeys are also available for your enjoyment. Prices are a little high, but well worth it. Reservations can be made by phone: 251-928-4321.

Camellia Café is closed Sunday and Monday and open from 5:00 p.m. until 10:00 p.m. the rest of the week. Choose this café and enjoy.

JW

Dragonfly Foodbar
7 South Church Street

The Dragonfly Foodbar is housed in a yellow building located at the corner of De la Mare and Church streets. The salads, smalls, tacos, bowls, and sides menus offer a variety of Mexican and Asian fusion of servings. There is much to choose from, including a Baby Spinach Salad, a Seared Tuna Taco, a Curry Roasted Lamb bowl, and a Cold Edamame side.

This writer was particularly impressed with the Crispy Oyster Blue Cheese Toast, a delicacy listed as a "Smalls" choice. It was absolutely delicious, well prepared with appealing presentation. Servers and bartenders are friendly and attentive. Outside and inside seating is available.

Customers have given Dragonfly Foodbar an overall five-star rating. Pricing is moderate, but a three percent charge is required for credit card payments. They prefer cash.

The Dragonfly Foodbar is open Monday through Saturday from 11a.m. to 9 p.m. and closed on Sunday. Their phone number is (251) 990-5722. Stop by and enjoy an interesting lunch or dinner.

JW

Fairhope Inn and Restaurant
63 South Church Street

After a recent outstanding renovation and extensive revamping of the grounds, this twenty-year-old establishment reopened its doors and is getting excellent to rave reviews. First of all, we love the small intimate feel of the place and their proximity to everything downtown.

Second of all, we hold dear the menu, limited as it is. Steaks and seafood are the rule of the day, with exceptional appetizers. We are partial to the beet salad with its orange slices, Gorgonzola cheese, and *crème fraiche.* My wife thought the Louisiana-Creole-inspired shrimp remoulade was next to perfection. From the entrees, I had the filet mignon with truffle mashed potatoes, and a wonderful braised fennel. My wife chose, as she always does, the grilled tasso encrusted salmon, polenta wedge, and roasted zucchini with a marvelous Hollandaise. Of course, they had to gild the lily, which is why the deserts are little works of art that defy anyone's description.

If you are here on Sunday, you can do no better than having your brunch here. Again, the menu is limited but what comes out of the kitchen and rushed to your table is inspired and looks to be fresh off the pages of *Gourmet Magazine.* Adore and seek out terrific service and a crisp white table cloth with standing napkins? Then you are in for an incomparable treat.

RM

Honeybaked Ham
Fairhope and Bancroft

While franchises are not encouraged here in Fairhope, Honeybaked Ham has been in its location at the corner of Fairhope Avenue and Bancroft Street for so many years, it seems like a town fixture.

The place is hopping (no pun intended) at Easter with locals lining up for their Easter hams and turkey breasts, but the café is a marvelous spot for a quick lunch. The ham and turkey are, of course, the main features, but soups and salads are also on the café menu. A kids' menu is available for your little ones.

Perhaps lesser known is Honeybaked's catering menu. They offer everything from full holiday dinners to go, to buffet trays and boxed lunches for your traveling events. Desserts, beverages, and delivery makes for a complete package. No work and DEE-licious!

RG

It's All Greek To Me!
108 N. Section Street

This bright, sunny little restaurant is located in a small set-back courtyard bordered by several other shops and restaurants. There are a few comfortable tables and chairs in the shared outdoor area, and ten or so inside the building. Their popularity combined with limited seating means reservations or a wait for dinner during the busy season.

They are not so busy at lunch, though. I had lunch there on a mild spring day, sitting outside in some shade. Within a couple of minutes, a waiter came over, presented the menu, made recommendations, took my order, and quickly came back with a fresh French press of coffee. After mashing the grounds to the bottom, the aroma gave notice that this was not just average coffee, which, indeed, proved to be the case. Unexpectedly exceptional is how I would put it.

In about ten minutes my order was placed on the table. Very nice! Spanakopita (a spinach and feta pie) with fries almost over filling the large plate, as it certainly would on a street corner in Athens. Hard to think of a more traditional dish. One of my favorites when I was on liberty from the ship in Greece.

Given the small size of their kitchen, I would think much of the cooking is done off site, but in any case they did a reasonable job. The flavor was spot on. Portion sizes were generous; many lighter eaters may well request a take away box.

It sure looks like "It's All Greek to Me!" is trying hard to be an authentic Greek sidewalk cafe. I hope they keep the emphasis on authenticity, as real Greek cuisine is hard to find but worth the effort.

They also have a good selection of beer and wine to complement your meal, of course.

The desserts looked delicious, although I did not have the time to try one.

Prices are what you might expect in a prime downtown Fairhope location. After all, they are not a burger joint!

All things considered, a nice, sunny, fairly authentic Greek restaurant with a cheerful atmosphere, quick smart service, and food that you will put on your "yes" list.

KJ

Julwin's
411 Fairhope Avenue

You know how it feels to wake up to the smell of fresh coffee and bacon and just be glad to be alive? Well, walking into Julwin's restaurant in downtown Fairhope is like that.

Opened in 1945, Julwin's is the oldest restaurant in Baldwin County, and they serve breakfast and happiness all day long. I have it on good authority that the blueberry pancakes are big, fluffy, and delicious. My personal joy is the thick-sliced bacon and hashbrowns that are cooked just right.

As good as breakfast is, though, a Blue Plate-style lunch is often just what the tummy is craving. Good Southern comfort food includes all the regular players from country fried steak to liver and onions. Of course, there are really good hamburgers, sandwiches, and salads, so everybody's happy.

Their regular hours are 6:30 a.m. to 2 p.m. (7:30 a.m. to 1 p.m. on Sundays), but once a month they have Steak Night. While they certainly have steak on Steak Night, Julwin's also offers up such culinary treats as lamb chops, sea scallops, and pan-seared grouper, along with appetizers, sides, and desserts. Keep a watch out for this; you need reservations, as it fills up fast

PP

Little Whiskey Christmas Club
14 North Church Street

Crazy, zany, and fun is one way to describe this one-of-a-kind bar. Yes, there are Christmas decorations everywhere twelve months out of the year, and yes they have a great selection of drinks. It can get a little loud in this eclectic establishment, but maybe that is why it is popular with fun loving folks. The menu is a notch above predictable bar food. No, you might not rave about it, but you won't send it back, because it fills the bill and there is plenty on your plate. Rumor has it most of the food is brought in from the Bone and Barrel Pub, which is its sister bar only forty feet away. This is a great place to watch a sports event and if you like sitting outside, they have a terrific deck under an enormous oak tree—sometimes with live music. Now and again, they spring for an AYCE crab, shrimp, and crawfish boil, which is exceptionally good. Happy Hour 3-7. Karaoke 9:30. Thursday, Friday, Saturday. Open till the wee hours.

RM

Locals
410 Fairhope Avenue

Wonderful, creative, and incredible food takes more time to prepare than that at an average diner, so be prepared for a bit longer wait for whatever memorable food you are about to eat. I'll start with what Wade and Ashley Peryer are famous for and that is burgers. Wow! Kangaroo, bison, alligator, wild boar, wildebeest, lamb, venison, elk, and other wild game. Well maybe not wildebeest, but you will be pleasantly surprised at the juicy complex flavors the chef can magically prepare in a small cramped kitchen.

Oh yes, he then serves this juiciness on a homemade ciabatta or focaccia roll that is the top and bottom of the whole extravaganza. Cheese? Yes, and it comes from that tiny little cheese farm everyone is talking about over in Elberta and down a red clay road. No, I haven't finished with the burgers. On top of the delightful cheese are sauces that vary each day. Mango, peach, green tomatoes, and caramelized home grown sweet onions are some of his favorites. Of course, the big-chunk, deep fried potato strips have been rolled in something secret and spicy to keep pace with the burgers.

But if you are not in the mood for a giant burger, try the shrimp and grits. A lot of my friends say they are the best in southern Alabama, although some purists say they may be a little teensy bit too rich. Most diners will admit privately they enjoy the uncommonly thick creamy sauce.

Ashley, who is the face of Locals, attempts to buy all her vegetables locally, which means your salad may have been picked early this morning over in Silverhill, eleven miles and a pickup truck ride away.

And if the chef was once a pastry chef, we would not be surprised. Again, like any good restaurant, the desserts change according to the ingredients the locals can serve up. Peach pudding? Maybe. Blackberry pie? Yes, if he can get someone to pick some. Blueberries? Always when in season. And if he is backed into a corner, out comes the carrot cake that has several special secret ingredients that make it unlike any other you have tried. Or the pecan bread pudding with an incredible rich whiskey sauce.

Locals is open at 11, so you might be able to get a late breakfast, and if you come later or Friday and Saturday nights you can BYOB. Check out the chalk board for daily specials—what you see there will be interesting and you'll not leave disappointed.

RM

Mary Ann's Deli
Inside The Mill, 85 N. Bancroft Street

Mary Ann's Deli has been a favorite for decades, for entertaining out-of-town guests and for great food. The selections are terrific! The menu flaunts twenty-three enjoyable sandwiches, nine scrumptious salads, and daily weekday specials for soups and quiche. A longtime favorite is the "Cosmopolitan Trio Salad" served with a choice of chicken, tuna, or shrimp salad, and two sides (of potato or pasta salad, coleslaw, pimiento cheese, fresh fruit, soup, or garden salad). Poppyseed dressing is fantastic, glazed over the fruit. It's a tradition!

Chef Bob Coppoletta says the most-often-ordered sandwich is the "Shirley," made of smoked turkey and provolone cheese with homemade honey mustard on grilled sourdough. A close runner-up is the "Michael T," somewhat similar to Shirley, but made with sliced grilled chicken breast on sourdough. As a culinary master, Bob's personal favorite is the New Orleans muffuletta, packed with ham, salami, provolone cheese, and mixed olive salad on seeded muffuletta bread. Drinks and sodas aren't usually an item to get excited about, but the mango peach sweet tea is worth the visit by itself. And the small inexpensive square of Mississippi Mud Cake is just enough to fill a sweet tooth without sinking the calorie ship!

Mary Ann's entrance door is on Equity Street, next to Nall's Art Studio, or you can enter through The Mill at 85 N. Bancroft Avenue. The quality value of Mary Ann's Deli, blended with the convenience of The Mill's optional food choices, make the Mill a must stop for visitors and residents alike.

RMG

Master Joe's
21 North Section Street

It is an old rule of thumb. If there is a line out the door, something good is happening on the other side. In this case, it is a respectable Japanese restaurant. Some would say more than respectable; some would say downright wonderful to have it here. Sushi is their specialty. And, by the comments we've heard over the years, this place should be landmarked. Ignore the spartan appearance, the long bench along the wall; ignore the noise of chattering happy diners. The selection is pretty wonderful, but the freshness of everything is remarkable. We usually opt for the sushi, but the menu offers some very nice meals from tempura to teriyaki. Sit at the long sushi bar and have a nice cold Japanese beer, or opt for an ale from a fairly good selection. Now watch their well-trained sushi magicians at work. We usually start with the miso soup, which is best sipped right out of the bowl, and move on to a terrific little salad, made with a dressing that consists of pureed apple and navel orange slices, sesame oil, and a few secret ingredients that taste like maybe a whisper of almond butter.

Sometimes, we just come for the salad and stay for the sushi. The lunch special we usually order has enough sushi for two. The ahi and yellow tail tuna still score high with my better half, and I prefer the California roll. So get there a little early to beat the crowd in the evening. At lunch, if you are there exactly at 12 noon, you should have no trouble getting a seat to enjoy reasonable prices, fast service, and the best Japanese cuisine in southern Alabama. One last thing, if you are looking for a Hibachi table with a chef that makes an onion look like a volcano, you won't find it here. Here, it is about the food.

RM

McSharry's Irish Pub
101 North Bancroft Street

In 2006, Ronan McSharry left his home in Sligo, Ireland, moved to Fairhope, and opened McSharry's Irish Pub. It quickly became a Gulf Coast favorite. A full bar and cozy dining room with sports TV is inside the pub and on the lovely "Paddy O" outside. The menu boasts a fine selection of authentic Irish dishes as well as local American favorites.

McSharry's is a great place to relax and unwind. There are live DJs on Friday and Saturday and sometimes local bands on other evenings and nights. Sunday  offers a very special musical experience. If you are settled in at the bar or a table around 6:00 to 6:30 p.m., enjoying your shepherd's pie or some other special dish and perhaps a Guinness stout, you will begin to notice folks walking past carrying musical instruments—violins, fiddles, flutes, mandolins, and others— filing in, one or maybe two at a time. They will gather and greet each other in the northeast end of the dining room. Soon, they will begin to tune their instruments. Then, for as long as two or three hours, they will play one Irish song after another, stopping only for an occasional drink or short break. Sometimes an authentic Irish tenor will join in. Some of the musicians are professionals from the Mobile and Pensacola symphonies, while others are just musicians who enjoy playing Irish tunes. They come from as far away as New Orleans. Their performances represent the longest running traditional Irish music sessions on the Gulf Coast, and they are a pleasure to hear. McSharry's bartenders and servers will continue to take and serve your food and drink orders while the music is playing.

You will enjoy your visit to McSharry's. And, of course, if you happen to be in Fairhope on Saint Patrick's Day, the celebration at McSharry's is the place to be.

JW

The Mill
85 N. Bancroft

The attractive metal building with open sides sat empty for years after an auto dealership closed at Equality and Bancroft. The environmentally friendly Windmill Market opened there about ten years ago and featured a deli, sandwich shop, and lots of small booths with paintings and wares, and a sign that simply said, "Put your payment in the cash box."

In 2018, the whole venue changed to "The Mill." The open space was reconfigured to a large casual eating space with three or four restaurant choices offering creative cuisine and a more open atmosphere. It now is home for several imaginative eateries, soft drinks, beer, and frozen treats that

appeal to quick, but not fast food, appetites in a pleasant uncrowded setting.

Cereal Killer is a coy way of saying "We have great selections that trample your routine morning cereal." Perhaps better described as a brunch spot, their Churro Bubble Waffle is inexpensive and fun-different. Sunny Shrimp Tacos crusted with corn flakes, or a crispy fried chicken "Croque Madame" are beyond a breakfast meal.

Mary Ann's Deli is also a part of The Mill family with its own lunch specialties. See a more detailed review on page 62.

The Ox Kitchen owners now nurture an organic menu of healthy foods. Their Grain Bowl scores well with the watchers of waistlines. The owners, Dennis and Elizabeth, are superb at friendly customer care.

Sundae School heads the class for ice cream and yogurt after finding your favorite entree at the other venues in The Mill.

Taps, along the west wall of the spacious dining area, allows the practicing beer aficionado to experiment with area ales or lagers in a pleasant well-lighted environment.

The new outdoor picnic tables under shelter on the south side of The Mill are a surprising and enjoyable reason to bring the kids along to eat and play on clean synthetic grass. Romping a little is permissible, and some soft happy squeals are okay. It's a super place to meet a friend or another mom with a stroller, or preschooler. Lunch hour will get busier but kids are always welcome. Businessmen with legal pads, nursing students with backpacks, and ladies meeting for business or a leisure lunch are regulars.

RMG

Panini Pete's

42 South Section Street

Some say he is a legend; others just say he is on his way to becoming a legend. Pete is about six feet five, and you can't miss the man. What he has brought here to Fairhope is the taste of New Orleans on a simpler scale. His breakfast panino is egg, cheese, and bacon on two pieces of toast that he passes his magic wand over and vaboom, it is heaven. But don't start there. Start with an order of beignets. Many say Café Du Monde has the best; we say, "Not so fast; have you tasted Panini Pete's beignets?" They are made and cooked fresh every five minutes.

Now stay for lunch and have a black and blue burger made with true prime black Angus beef, the best blue cheese around, and a blackened sauce born deep in a mysterious bayou somewhere north of New Orleans. Yes, there is a line for lunch, but it moves fast. Or get here a few minutes before noon. Eat outside under a ninety-year-old oak tree, or dine in the green glass atrium Pete discovered and crated in from Disney World.

Service is fast and the servers are bright and cheery. It's not open for dinner, but he has another restaurant near town that is a short drive away and has a great view of the bay and marina. It's called Sunset Pointe; we love it too. His downtown restaurant opens at 8 a.m. and closes about two or so.   *RM*

R Bistro and Bakery

334 Fairhope Avenue

Sometimes you are so happy about a restaurant you want to jump up and down. R Bistro proudly proclaims it is somewhat French/American/Creole/Cajun. We say amen to that. The always present owner, Joe Rider, circulates, catering to your every desire, and ready with a funny remark while you dine. Yes, it is a gem, and yes, it is hidden in plain sight. Here are some of surprises that will delight you here. An incredible Croque Monsieur, fabulous bacon wrapped scallops, a melt in your mouth with perfect crust quiche, a fantastic shrimp po'boy, tasty tenderloin sliders, a gumbo made in heaven, and Dixie shrimp that look incredible and taste better than they look. Wait there is more! If that's not enough, how about a true rich European coffee to go with that crème brûlée or caramel cake or peanut butter pie? The chef has many offers on the table from some of the top restaurants in New Orleans, but has chosen to live here. Thank goodness. The service is excellent. This is an intimate restaurant and so you should adjust accordingly. We usually sit at the marble bar and enjoy the view of passersby.

R Bistro is open 11 to 3 for lunch; on Fridays and Saturdays they stay open for dinner until 9. Yes, the menu is limited but everything is wonderfully made and wonderfully presented, and each dish dances wonderfully on your tongue. Don't miss it.

RM

Ravenite Pizza

102 North Section Street

Ravenite   Pizzeria specializes in New York style thin and crispy pizza, but the menu also includes calzones,   wings,   salads, and pasta.

Bring the family and/or friends for nights of Live Trivia, Rock 'n Roll Bingo, and Karaoke. For the weekend night owls, *Ravenite* stays open till 2 a.m. on Friday and Saturday nights. Open at 11 a.m. Mon-Sat and 4 p.m. on Sunday.

Dine in or carry out. Moderately priced.

RG

Sage Lebanese Cuisine and Café

319 Fairhope Avenue

Sage is an intimate, relaxed eatery in the heart of downtown Fairhope with a unique and delicious menu, offering both Lebanese specialties and Mediterranean dishes.

Start with the Meza Mixer appetizer which includes samplings of hummus, labneh, moussaka, stuffed grape leaves, and falafel with warm pita bread. And isn't it fun just to say, "falafel?"

Salads and pita sandwiches appear on the menu for a lighter appetite, but favorites with me and mine are the scrumptiously marinated chicken or beef kabobs served with a yummy garlic sauce and rice. My guy claims Sage has the best lamb chops he has ever had.

On any of Fairhope's perfect weather days, a couple of sidewalk tables give an upfront view of the passing folks. Come in and dine for either lunch or dinner. Moderately priced.

RG

Sandra's Place Deli
218 Fairhope Avenue

Just steps from the corner of Church Street and Fairhope Avenue, hungry folks will find Sandra's Place. A palette of

colorful umbrellas marks the spot. Nestled comfortably at a table on the outdoor brick patio, diners at Sandra's can observe the rhythm of life as it moves up and down busy Fairhope Avenue. Sandra's bills itself as "A Friendly Southern Deli," and, indeed, that is the feeling one gets when entering the small indoor space at 218 Fairhope Avenue. The building is charming in itself with its angled location and lighthouse cupola. The outdoor patio beckons tourists and locals alike to come in for a bit of time out of the sun and a hearty sandwich, salad, or soup offering. Even on a crisp day in Fairhope, a see-through plastic shield protects patio tables from the breeze.

Sandra Whitley has been at this location for more than twenty years, at first opening in the indoor space with coffee, cookies, and gourmet candies. At the suggestion of a regular, she increased her menu and offered a specialty sandwich each day. Now the menu has expanded to dozens of offerings, including a daily special sandwich and soup. In the winter, there are two or three soups on the board. Sandra told this writer that her chicken salad is "world famous." She can make the claim because her brother-in-law heard someone bragging about it when he visited Ireland some years ago!

Desserts, cakes, pies, and cookies are made on-site each day. Everything is made fresh in their tiny "two-butt" kitchen. Customers can also take home the chicken, egg, tuna, pimento cheese, pasta, and fruit salads by the pound.

Sandra now does the bookwork for the business, and her daughter, Lisa Bates, has taken over the day-to-day operation as manager. The staff is made up of part-timers who are native Fairhopians and others from all over the world. The clientele is national and international as well. Senators, mayors, governors, authors, and actors have occupied tables at the deli.

The town of Fairhope has grown and prospered these past few decades, and Sandra's is proud to be a part of that, serving up good food and friendly service, adding to the town's reputation as a must-see day stop for our many Gulf Coast tourists, and a mainstay for all of the local customers.

When you're hungry for lunch in Fairhope, you can't go wrong with a stop at Sandra's Place Deli. The food is a delight and the smiles are friendly. Sit yourself under a Sandra's umbrella and watch Fairhope pass by. Y'all come.

RG

Section Street Pizza
108 North Section Street

I love easy reviews of great restaurants. Section Street Pizza certainly fills that bill.

They are located in the same shared courtyard near "It's All Greek To Me!" This is a nice, shady, laid back spot to bring your girlfriend, kids, or dogs, and have a relaxed lunch or dinner.

Inside it is cool, bright, and well-lit with large windows and good views, and the seats and tables are comfortable. There are not so many tables that the place feels crowded, even during a busy lunch.

The aromas coming from the oven sharpen your appetite, so that even if you weren't that hungry, by the time you start looking at a menu, you certainly will be!

I ordered a pizza with a lot of veggies the first time. It was fantastic, one of the best veggie pizzas I have ever had. The flavor was terrific, and the crust was perfect, crisp with no hint of sogginess, which seems to be hard for many pizza makers to achieve on a veggie pizza.

I have also tried one of their pizzas with sausage and pepperoni. It was perfect. It probably is the combination of the brick oven and homemade dough, but whatever, it is great! The sauce was just right also, intense, flavorful, tangy, but not a bit watery—or worse, greasy.

I understand they also make very nice salads from fresh produce. That will have to wait for another day, hopefully soon.

As I was leaving, I noted that one last thing—you get a top quality, superior pizza, but you do not pay a boutique price. My kind of place.

Section Street Pizza is located just across the street from the police station in downtown Fairhope. They are open 11 a.m. to 9 p.m. every day except Monday.

KJ

Tamara's Downtown
104 North Section Street

One reason we love this place is the building itself. Its tall, barreled ceiling—burned in places from a fire in the 1950s—gives a feeling of grand dining places in the old world. And maybe that is what Tamara thought of when she opened the place and designed the menu. They pride themselves on being a little bit Tuscan, and a little bit New Orleans. They did both under one roof. The bar is possibly the best large bar around, with hints of bars from the 1930s. Big. Bold. Brassy.

The dining room, separated only by the thin screen of lattice work, is wide and spacious. If you want to be seen, this is the place to go. There is no hiding in a quiet corner with small talk. In other words, it is not a romantic hideaway for young lovers— for that, you go across the street to the Camellia Café. But back to Tamara's Downtown and to why we came in the first place. That would be the food. Seafood or steaks or pasta. It is that simple, but the devil is in the details. Shrimp and grits is not Tuscan, but it is New Orleans, and it is a favorite of many because she does it so well. Other seafood items include pan fried sea scallops over a bed of wilted spinach with parmesan risotto. Encrusted grouper with Gouda mashed potatoes and three-cheese crab moray. All have been wonderful in the past.

As for the steaks, the prime rib is a standout; it is certified Angus beef and comes with the necessary horseradish, fresh broccoli or carrots, and tri-colored potatoes. All steaks are hand cut and what you would expect from a woman who prides herself on tenderness.

Tamara's is also a good place for lunch, with fresh ground hamburger paired with what appears to be enough potato fries for two hungry eaters. They also have other lunch specials that change daily; just check the chalk board for what is cooking out in the kitchen. The wine list is fitting for a place this large and this varied in offerings. They have a website that reveals a lot more than we can cover here. If you catch Tamara out in the kitchen doing her own cooking, you are in for a treat. She knows her stuff.

RM

Texarbama BBQ
212 ½ Fairhope Avenue

OK, the first thing to know about Texarbama BBQ is how to get there. It is in a back alley off Fairhope Avenue. Just keep Running Wild on your left as you proceed down the narrow way and in a hundred feet you will see, and probably smell, Texarbama BBQ.

There is some open-air seating outside, mainly for those who want a nice Cuban cigar with their meal, I think, or for people like me when I show up on my bicycle but with no lock so want to keep an eye on it.

Once inside, you may think someone transported a Texas roadhouse to downtown Fairhope. It certainly has that feel. They even have a jukebox in the corner, right next to the well-stocked bar. Never could see how those Texans managed to dance so well wearing those cowboy boots; maybe it is the whiskey, after all. Besides the jukebox, they do have live music from time to time.

I tried the beef brisket. You can get quarter, half, or full pound servings of meat; I had a half pound. It was really good, very tender with that smoky barbecue flavor. Sides are charged separately. I ordered jalapeno lime cole slaw, which was fresh, unique, and delicious. I also added a baked potato, of which they have several varieties. I was tempted to try the Frito pie, but did not as I had a LOT of brisket. Maybe next time.

I know their collards are great, people rave about their BBQ tacos, and they have bacon cookies. WOW!

My only complaint was I would prefer something other than just a plastic tray to eat the food off of. I know it's down-home, but still.

They are family friendly; every time I have been there, two or three couples with kids fill the bench seating area. Those look like one I had in my '59 Buick. They are open 10 a.m. - 11 p.m., Tuesday through Sunday. Closed Monday.

KJ

Thyme on Section
33 N. Section Street

Thyme on Section is another in a growing group of fine restaurants in Fairhope. Occupying a smallish space that was once an antique store, the upscale décor is several notches above their previous cottage location. The hip interior allows diners to view the three chefs through a large picture window as they prepare some of the most innovative gastronomic creations here in our small town.

The lunch menu offers burgers, gyros, and pastrami sandwiches. Traveling upward on the menu are the mahi fish and chips, and bistro mussels. Dinner steps it up a bit. The Caesar salad, with their own house-cured bacon and herb goat cheese, is a great starter for dinner. The manti pasta with Turkish seasoned lamb, charred onion, grape tomatoes, baby carrots, and toasted pistachio caught my eye. But don't overlook the butternut squash risotto with roasted apple, pecan, rosemary, and apple brandy jus.

Brunch on Sundays is a little out of the ordinary. The eggs Benedict with crab come with a rich puree of avocado and a coup de grâce hollandaise, all sitting on a crunchy sourdough. Not far behind is their fresh berry buttermilk pancakes with vanilla bean cream.

For such a small restaurant, Thyme on Section has a complex menu, offering generous portions for moderate prices. The menu may change daily to reflect availability of produce and seasonality of dishes.

Hours are: Tuesday through Saturday 11-3 for lunch and 5-9 for dinner. Sunday brunch is 10:30 to 3, with Sunday dinner from 5-9. Closed Mondays. Limited Reservations. Call 251-990-5635.

RM

Wok By D'Bay

420 Fairhope Avenue

This is a long awaited and beautifully designed restaurant that promised fine Chinese dining, but, alas, it is a hit or miss experience. Sometimes service is fast and sometimes it is slow; sometimes the food is wonderful and sometimes it is boring and bland. Yes, the menu reads Chinese Fusion, but many times it misses the mark. The lunch menu is filled with soups that range from wonton soup to Pad Thai and about eight more. We did find the beef teriyaki measured up to our standards and the Kung Pao chicken was quite tasty. In the evening we enjoyed the Mongolian beef and the Peking duck. But the uneven service and long wait times should not be tolerated. All we can say is that every time we dine there the service and offerings seem to be getting better. Cross your fingers. *RM*

Weather

Boy, oh boy, do we have weather here, and there is plenty to go around. First and foremost, keep in mind we are near the subtropics, so we have subtropical weather similar to when you are on vacation in Fiji, or Hawaii, or the Virgin Islands. Which means tropical rain can fall on one side of the street and not fall where you are standing, or vice versa. We also have a little gift called humidity. It may cause you to perspire, which is a natural way of cooling yourself. But being close to the Gulf of Mexico and Mobile Bay, we also have a bay breeze cooling everybody.

Now, you people from Arizona, our Alabama sun is never so hot as to burn a hole in your hat, because we have clouds that cover the sun and help us through the day. Summer usually starts about the first of June and meanders slowly into about the middle of September. We won't talk about July or August, except to say we invented sweet iced tea for a good reason.

Then comes wonderful fall, with highs in the seventies and lows in the fifties, and everyone gets out a little windbreaker and talks about football games on Saturday and trick-or-treat and Thanksgiving. Trees drop their leaves, and the flowers around town are changed out to marigolds and mums. This, I call our California weather.

Winter comes after the lighting of the trees in downtown Fairhope, and it can be downright cold out there. For our snowbird friends dropping out of the freezing northern states, highs will be mostly in the sixties—sometimes higher, sometimes lower—depending on the whims of the Weather Man. We can experience frosts at this time of year, but once the sun comes out, everybody seems happy. You may want mittens for the late evening, but only if you are out for extended periods. Camellias remind us that red and green are the true Christmas colors, and do it with style, sparing no expense to impress us during this time.

Spring is like fall with similar California weather, only now, the trees are making bright green new leaves and the sun feels good on our faces. The fashion trend is back to shorts and tee shirts. We will get stronger breezes off the bay, and that can make for white caps down on the water. It is at this time that the Azaleas come out in glorious displays and about everyone in Fairhope has at least ten planted in front of their homes, so it is a divine pink, red, and white explosion that Walt Disney could not have planned better in Technicolor.

Don't forget your umbrella! We get more rain than most any place else in the forty-eight states. Mobile is usually the U.S. champion with, on average, eighty-five inches a year. We also have incredible lightning strikes, along with her twin sister thunder. At times it will rattle your teeth. If the lightning is really close to you, go inside for a while and it will pass. Beedee Burkmeister, the only person in Fairhope ever hit by lightning, says it was a little like seeing a Fourth of July fireworks show, but all at once and about three feet away. She claims she can now see in the dark and has thrown away her glasses. Her husband says she cooks better too.

RM

Shopping

De la Mare Avenue

In spite of its romantic-sounding name, De la Mare Avenue is really named after a long-time resident and entrepreneur who established two large glass greenhouses on the property. The street was little more than an alley. When the growing city closed in on him, Mr. De la Mare packed up his glass panels and left town, leaving only a street name as verification of his presence in Fairhope. Just a block long, De la Mare Avenue is packed with places to browse.

Beginning just behind the *Page and Palette* book store corner, the *Lyons Share Gallery* features the work of over fifty local and regional artists, as well as offering a vast selection of frames and framing services. The design of the shop is clever and contemporary. A staircase, which could dominate the space, appears to float, with see-through risers and railings. A different artist is featured each month, debuting on Art Walk Night. Mike and Kelley Lyons like to find artists whose work tells a story and piques the interest of their customers.

Next door at *In the Company of Angels,* you'll find a celestial stop filled with gift ideas for babies, for angel lovers and collectors, or for an inspirational or comforting gift for anyone who may be in need of a morale booster. You can also pick up a special something for readers, gardeners, and people of faith.

Southern Gents is a casual boutique for men to balance out the many women's clothiers and give the guys an excuse to treat themselves to new duds. Some of their brand offers are: Drake, Properly Tied, Genteal, and Vineyard Vines.

For foodies, *The Happy Olive* is an essential stop. Here, one can sip and taste dozens of imported, flavor-infused olive oils and balsamic vinegars to enhance any dish. Assemble a gift box sure to please with small bottles in a variety of flavors. Many other fun and unusual kitchen accoutrements are also on display. In the words of one of their employees, the store is "a field trip for adults"—especially those who love to cook.

B Southern is a ladies' boutique flanking a corner of the De La Mare entrance to the *French Quarter.* They feature quality clothing at a reasonable price that you won't find everywhere else you look. Brands include Free People, Sundays, Dear John, and more.

CK Men's Collection is the next stop on the De la Mare tour. If you gents are feeling slighted by the lack of men's wear on Fairhope Avenue, pop into CK's to check out fabulous upscale clothing and shoes for you. Some of the brands are: Peter Millar, Scott Barner, Barbour, Mizzen & Main, and many more.

By now you may be in need of a rest and a pick-me-up, and the porch at *Mr. Gene's Beans* is the place to rest your tootsies and enjoy an ice cream treat or a hot cup of specialty coffee. Gourmet popcorn is available. Relax under a protective umbrella outdoors or at a cozy table inside.

After your rest, cross the street to meander among the north side shops.

The Fairhope Soap Company offers soaps, candles, candle warmers, unique towels, and bath accessories, including moisturizing bath bombs. For him, there is a line of shaving and beard accessories. Everything is handmade in house, with no toxic ingredients.

At *The Little Drawer,* you may browse a selection of luxurious sleepwear and lingerie. The shop also has a bra fit specialist to help you get just the comfort level you've been looking for.

Estate Jewelers features fine jewelry, collectible jewelry, and wearable art.

Don't miss a browse at *The Copper Column* gallery. Begin with a walk through an arbor and enter the shop for a stunning eclectic variety of artwork, including something called bottle cap art. A sensual delight wherever you look. Everything from ball gowns to fashion jewelry to architectural antiques—a collection that is impossible to duplicate or describe.

Next stop is *Aubergine.* Culinary antiques with a French flavor, antique sideboards, custom-made European tables, and imported chandeliers are artfully arranged to please the eye and tempt the shopper. There is a collection of Oriental rugs available as well.

The Fairhope Store shouldn't be missed by either tourist or resident. Proclaim your love for our little town in the form of a tastefully logoed tee shirt, fleece sweatshirt, cap, or tote bag. Each item is embellished with a subtle image of the Fairhope pier and waterfront, with dozens of colors and styles to choose from. Bicycles are available for rental for a tour around town on two wheels.

Last stop on our De la Mare tour is the *Red or White* shop, a wine store and tasting room. There is also a selection of craft beers, making this a marvelous late afternoon stop for a relaxing glass of vintage wine and a tasty nibble. Handmade pizzas and charcuterie (a fancy word for gourmet meat and cheese plates) are served Tuesday through Saturday from 3-8 p.m. Wine tastings are held every Saturday afternoon from 3-6 p.m.

So much to see on this block, just a tiche off the beaten paths of the main streets.

RG

Lagniappe

There is a Lot to See on Church Street—Just No Churches

If churches are your thing, whether for architecture or spiritual efficacy, Fairhope has plenty of them. Just don't go looking for them on Church Street.

Now Church Street has plenty to offer, from its beginning at the Fairhope Colony Cemetery (should that be the end?) at the corner of Oak and Church to its abrupt end at Fig Avenue. A 1.2-mile walk takes you through a lovely residential area, built in the late 1800s and early 1900s. The homes are well maintained with landscaped yards and flower beds at every turn.

At Magnolia Avenue, the area turns from residential to business, the beginning edge of downtown. Still, the beautifully tended profuse flower beds are on every corner, complementing the boutiques, businesses, and restaurants. If the walk makes you hungry, stop in at Sandra's Place, or Bay Breeze Café, or Fairhope Inn and Restaurant.

You can sit, rest, and digest in the large colorful park across from the quaint and picturesque building housing a community theatre. Closer inspection reveals this at least was *once* a church.

There, the area again turns residential, with a mix of graceful, perhaps more modest homes, interspersed with more imposing but newer structures.

If your goal, however, is to find a church, Fairhope is home to many great churches. We have selected the four that are located downtown and in walking distance of each other, neatly spaced on South Section Street.

PP

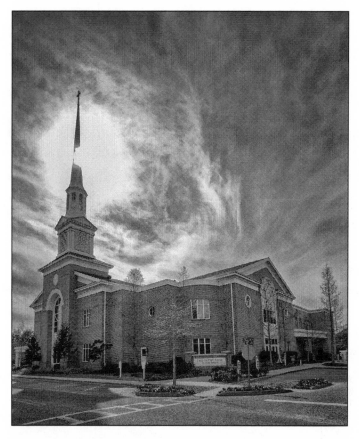

First Baptist Church-Fairhope 300 South Section Street. 251-928-8685. Sunday 8:30, 11:00 and 6.

Fairhope United Methodist
155 South Section Street. 251-928-1148. Services Sunday 8:30 and 11:00.

Redeemer Lutheran Church
200 South Section Street. 251-928-8397. Sunday 7:30 and 10.

St. Lawrence Catholic Church 370 South Section Street. 251-928-5931. Sat 5:30. Sunday 8:30, 11:00, and 5:30.

Gift Shops

Christmas Round the Corner
398 Fairhope Avenue

The customer who takes the exit from inside the Fairhope Pharmacy or enters from the street entrance must suddenly feel transported to a dazzling fairyland forest of seventeen eight- to-ten-foot trees glistening with hundreds of blown glass, resin, or fabric ornaments.

The idea for the Christmas shop was conceived when Betty Barnhill toured European countries in the 1970s and discovered shops dedicated to Christmas and filled with hand-blown ornaments of endless variety. Her daughter, Lou Anne Harrell, is the proprietor who will graciously assist you in browsing the shop and provide information on the trees and their contents.

Each tree is based on a theme or subject. Many contain collectible ornaments made by certain craftsmen, such as "Radko," and are asked for by name. The arrangement of trees in the middle, more like a Christmas forest, gets changed out from time to time, but always remains special and a sight to see.

Examples of the beautifully decorated trees you may find around this particular corner are *Old World Glass,* and the *Santa* tree. The *Victorian* tree is filled with ornaments illustrating Victorian styles. The glass type is called Egypteak. Many of these ornaments show gold overlay or are accented with 24K gold.

For those who celebrate with wine, the *Wine-Grape* tree is decked out with wine glasses and wine bottles in ornaments of various sizes. The *Bling* tree has shoes, purses, and lipsticks in sparkles and colors.

For the outdoor habitué there is the *Woodland* tree with glass animals, birds, and pine cones made of burlap and other fabrics.

The *Mardi Gras* tree shows typical objects in lots of color and bling. The *Garden* motif tree contains flowers and butterflies.

Of course, there is a *Dog* tree resplendent with every breed and size. The *Ballerina* has some ornaments in glass and some in fabric. Sports fans will like the *Sports* tree with porcelain ornaments by Haus in balls, motorcycles, and collegiate items. The popular *Fairhope* tree contains ships, boats, and shells.

In addition to angels, the *Angel* tree contains crosses and nativity glass ornaments. A *Hunting and Fishing* tree boasts horses, eagles, guns, and fishing rods. The *Music* tree has all kinds of instruments, including piano, violins, and guitars.

Recently they have added more metallic trees. Special ones are the "undersea trees, white with a blue light." The largest is six feet, but also there are all sizes to pick from.

Helen Doyle, a local artist, has contributed to another variety: local scenes on ornaments and key rings. The pier, fish, and crabs are a perennial favorite. Lou Anne stated the clock ornament is a new favorite, as well as the driftwood group of trees.

Most requested are the collectible ornaments *Radko,* blown glass, and *Egypteak.*

In addition to the trees, there are various figurines and ornamental structures set around the shop. You will find fairies and elves by Mark Roberts. Halloween witches fly from the ceiling. Easter Bunnies sit on ledges and tables. There are Fontannini and figurines of resin, also acrylic Nativity ornaments. An alligator ornament is a bottle topper.

There are decorative ribbons for any occasion. One can find Luminaria candles, electro-magnetic lighted flames and, of course, decorative wreaths and garlands. There are flags and banners, and ornamental creations for walls and doors.

It seems customary for merchants to promote the theme Christmas in July. Harrell commented, "I think customers can only tolerate six months of spring and summer, so they start dreaming of Christmas for relief." Further, she said, "The hotter it gets, I've noticed, the more people start buying for Christmas."

Certainly the store, with the crystalline effects of its dozens of trees and thousands of painted ornaments, induces the feeling of Christmas.

All the innovations assure the customers—tourists and natives—Christmas is just around the corner.

JM

The Church Mouse
14 South Church St.

What do fly fishing and English antiques have in common? If you are in Fairhope, the answer is the Church Mouse.

Housed in an eye-catching stone Cotswold cottage exterior, the Church Mouse carries an inventory of carefully selected antiques, gift items, English teas and biscuits—and hand-tied fishing lures.

The combination actually works very well. In the front of the store, murals of an English village, painted by Alabama artist Faye Earnest, grace the walls. The shelves and display cases proffer delicate tea pots, antique serving dishes, novelties, Sheffield silver, and more. Here and there a spot of bright color may reveal a card of poppers, perfect for catching some speckled trout or redfish.

The lures are hand tied by Spencer Johnson, co-owner of the Church Mouse with his wife, Mary Ann. Spencer is the artisan who crafts the lures and gives fresh and saltwater fly tying classes throughout the year.

The back of the store is devoted to sports clothing, fishing gear, a wide assortment of rods, Tilley hats, and, of course, fly fishing lures and fly tying supplies. The division is equitable; just as the lures were interspersed among the Royal Doulton pieces and French paté dishes, back here, antiques nestle comfortably among the fishing paraphernalia.

If you find yourself in the mood for some English teas from Taylors of Harrogate and a box of Weetabix or maybe some brandy butter, stroll down Church Street to the Church Mouse. You might even get a chance to witness one of Spencer Johnson's impromptu casting demonstrations.

Store hours are 10 a.m. to 5 p.m.

PP

Living Well
25 A South Section Street

We call this a decorating slash gift store because it seems to fit two purposes. You will find sophisticated and trendy offerings of accent pieces for yours or somebody else's home. They carry Matouk, Bellahotte, Gabby Interiors, Taylor Burke, Gigi NY, Nest candles, MB Green, and Branche. They also have a nice collection of original art, barware, lamps, and some chandeliers to dazzle your imagination. Open 10 to 5 daily.

RM

Ole Bay Mercantile
231 Fairhope Avenue

Set back from the busy street at the corner of Fairhope Avenue and Church Street, weary visitors can find relief on one of several benches set out for shoppers to stop and rest. The outdoor speakers pump out lively music to hum along to as shoppers stroll by. The window display offers a potpourri of decorative items, luring the browsing tourist, as well as local resident, inside.

Ole Bay Mercantile has a vast selection of gift and home accessory items in every price range—hats, beach bags, silk flower arrangements, scented as well as flameless candles, lamps, and serving pieces, many with a seaside theme. You'll find a collection of unique and adorable salt and pepper shakers. There are many corners to explore, and each offers its own surprise and delight. You may find wine accessories in one spot, fashion jewelry in another. Along one wall, I discovered a truly hilarious display of tea towels with outrageous sayings. As I passed one browser, she was standing in front of the table laughing hysterically. During any holiday season, customers can find a vast seasonal display of merchandise.

I brought a visiting friend in one day and she found the perfect lamp for her ocean-side cottage. The helpful staff aided her in arranging for shipping to her home on Cape Cod.

Whether searching for a gift for a hostess, wedding, birthday, or just a gift for yourself, you can no doubt find it while wandering the aisles of Ole Bay Mercantile.

RG

The Picture Show

332 Fairhope Avenue

I went to the picture show . . . no, not a movie, "The Picture Show," a little shop on Fairhope Avenue that bills itself as a card and stationery seller.

Only when I got there, I found they have so much more than just cards and stationery. They do have those items, but they also have pictures, picture frames, costume jewelry (the very glittery variety), interior decor, *objets d'art*, custom Christmas lights, and even scented candles. Perfumed might be more specific.

A collection in a small shop that will hold your interest for some time, even on a beautiful fall day.

Drop by and do your own investigating next time you are on Fairhope Avenue. You may find just what you were looking for, and didn't know it!

KJ

Poppins

315 Fairhope Avenue

Laura Fletcher has opened a menagerie of a gift shop in what is the smallest yet most intimate store in town. "I am forever searching for artisans here in the South willing to share their handmade crafts and art," says Laura. In other words, you will find one-of-a-kind, exciting, and wonderful items here. Yes, it is a tiny spot—but with big surprises. In the summer you might get free ice cold lemonade as you shop.

RM

River Bend
25 C South Section Street

River Bend is an unusual store in that it is a gift store for men. In other words, this is the place to buy a gift for your man. There should be a fireplace with a few logs and someone sitting by it smoking a pipe and sipping a twelve-year-old scotch.

They feature the best collection of walking sticks we have seen in a while, along with wonderfully made State-Tradition leather wallets, belts, watches, pocket knives, and don't miss the Kooringal hats. River Bend is also known for their Southern Marsh and Southern Point shirts and shorts. Warren Slay, the owner, has a great sense of what men appreciate and displays it with style. Ernest Hemingway would shop here.

RM

Jewelers

Brennys Jewelry
333 Fairhope Avenue

Brennys Jewelry, an elegant store on downtown Fairhope Avenue, is modeled after Tiffany and other luxury boutiques, with its hardwood floors, antique cherry jewelry cases, and Waterford chandeliers. It has served customers in a wide-ranging variety of ways since 1986.

Richard "Rick" Brenny, owner; Bill Hill, jeweler; and Mr. Brenny's son, Michael Brenny—CGA, certified gemologist and appraiser—research the jewelry market to find premier stones and one-of-a-kind items. They offer engraving and designing, and work with customers to create individualized heirlooms, restore old pieces, and create new ones from customers' own jewelry.

The scope of jewelry is extensive, with diamonds prevailing in all expressions: bracelets, rings, spectacular pendants, and necklaces. Gabriel diamond engagement rings, available in over 2,000 styles, are the newest and most sought after brand Brennys offers.

Rare colored stones are featured: rubies, sapphires, emeralds, and Alexandrite, as well as a variety of all popular colored gem stones. Brennys carries Brad Garmin pieces, hand crafted in Bangkok with fine, beautiful jewels. Customers will be glad to know there are diamond earrings in all sizes of 14K and 18K gold, and platinum.

There is a large collection of antique and vintage jewelry acquired from individuals and estates, and rarities from around the world, dating back to the early 1900s. One can find elegant but simply designed jewelry. Pearls include AAA (Triple A). Rolex watches, pre-owned but in new condition are offered at "old prices," Mr. Brenny said. A rare 40.2-carat stone from a far off island is on display inside a free-standing glass case. There are several glass-encased wall cabinets displaying a variety of jewels. Mr. Brenny encourages patrons to "come and see what's new that's old."

Discussions with Mr. Brenny reveal his lifelong enjoyment as a jeweler from his early experiences as a fifteen-year-old in his first job in a jewelry store, the experiences gained from work, corporate manufacturing, and as a traveling salesman, and finally, opening his store in Fairhope. This type of experience is rare among jewelry store owners and personnel and speaks to the expertise of Mr. Brenny.

His excitement and love for the beauty of stones and the art of creating jewelry, begun as a youth, is evident as one listens to stories of his work with customers to fulfill their desires for unique and individualized pieces.

The influences of his background growing up in a close, traditional family in the small town of Ferndale, Michigan, comes through as one observes his relationships with his employees and customers. He speaks eagerly of his desire to fulfill customers' requests to recreate a lost family heirloom or refashion an earlier design.

There are fourteen employees who say working at Brennys is like being part of a family. There is an on-site watch repairman, a specialist rarely found in today's jewelry stores. Brennys also offers engraving and appraisals.

Among newer items are Swiss-made Luminous watches, Seiko watches, Alamea sea jewelry from Hawaii, and Nomination sterling jewelry handmade in Florence, Italy.

Step into the bright, but warm, atmosphere of Brennys Jewelry Store and leisurely observe the many and diverse examples of the extravagantly beautiful jewelry, artfully displayed. Then go next door to Brennys Too and treat yourself to a stroll among the thousands of pieces of jewelry "created for quality and fun."

Brennys Too
331 Fairhope Avenue

As I entered Brennys Too, next door to Brennys Jewelry, I understood what Mr. Brenny meant by describing the store as "created for quality and fun." It must have been fun for him to conceive of creating a store of fashion jewelry with the quality and beauty offered in Brennys Too.

It has taken over a century for the beauty and quality of simulated diamonds to advance beyond that of costume jewelry. The term "costume jewelry" came into being after a German inventor in the late nineteenth century created rhinestones. There were stones made of glass and underlain by gold or silver foil material which emulated the sparkle and color of white diamonds. They came into prominence when Coco Chanel placed a rhinestone brooch on a dress for sale. Dress is *costume* in French. She commissioned designers at Cartier to fashion pins and various ornaments which would be pinned or sewn on her garments. Her action led to the custom of imitation gems being worn by ladies traveling, while leaving their expensive, genuine jewelry safely at home. Soon Hollywood designers recognized the value of using rhinestones to adorn the lavish gowns and costumes in movies featuring royalty or wealthy subjects. White rhinestones and colored versions were popular in the forties and fifties and were sold in department stores. Synthetic manufactured colored stones to resemble rubies, sapphires, emeralds, and citrines soon followed, but at the time it was not possible to manufacture the diamond. The introduction of the Cubic Zirconium (CZ) followed in white and all colors and shapes.

Meanwhile, Swarovski Crystals, a superior form of glass, remained popular from the early twentieth century to the present.

I was dazzled by a large glass case display of simulated diamonds to the right, just inside the store. Bright, white sparkling diamond solitaires, cluster earrings, and pendants were featured. A small display sign informed me that I was seeing "Lafonn's Laissaire" simulated diamonds. These contain the same physical properties as Cubic Zirconium, but are grown at a higher temperature, and therefore have a superior hardness and appearance to the average CZ found in the market. I knew at once this was a new and different simulated diamond. Next to the first large case was another display of rings, earrings, and pendants encased in platinum Lassaire and sterling.

Another case nearby featured natural colored stones—garnets, amethysts, and blue topaz—some of which were encased in 14K gold-filled, a time-honored gold metal more durable than gold-plated or gold-toned. There are 14K gold-filled and sterling charms.

Yet another case displayed a variety of Lassaire diamond earrings as well as diamond and pearl earrings and necklaces.

Moving on, I was surprised to see a stunning display of hand-carved, one-of-a-kind large cameos with natural stones arranged artistically at the perimeter. These cameos are the work of Allasandro, the foremost carver of cameos in Italy. I have always favored cameos and spectacular is the word I would apply to these beauties.

Another distinctive ensemble consisted of cream-colored enamel large bracelets with CZs. They are tagged "Bellaforth" diamond and enamel bracelets.

A metals display included necklaces of stones and sterling. A unique type of jewelry exhibited is the popular petite style of necklace known as the "Y" in 14K and a tiny diamond. There was a variety of the ever-popular necklaces and earrings in freshwater pearls fastened with classic 14K gold clasps.

I was glad to learn that Brennys employs a specialist who repairs broken strings of pearls and will re-string or re-knot pearl necklaces. This is good news for those of us with set-aside necklaces in need of repair.

An unusual display featured Byzantine crosses of bronze, rimmed in gold or silver. These are certified authentic, dated 324-640 A.D.

Mothers, grandmothers, and aunts will be pleased to see a large collection of jewelry for the baby in all types of rings, bracelets, earrings, and bar pins.

The store offered one surprise after another. There is an interesting collection of Jackie Kennedy jewelry: bracelets, necklaces, and pearls, all accompanied with documentation describing the occasions when her pieces were worn.

A very large wall and display case featured Pandora jewelry, rated as the number one designer jewelry worldwide. The popular Pandora bracelet and necklace are imaginative variations of the early Victorian era charm bracelet and slide-chain charm necklaces. These are to be had in necklace, bracelet, or earring form and in gold and sterling, CZs, or diamonds. Buying one at a time, a person can create individualized jewelry.

A display of Kovel jewelry offered enamel and silver one-of-a-kind pendants crafted by William Shraft, a designer formerly with David Yurman.

When you visit Brennys Too, you can be assured of an interesting diversion, and an opportunity to choose an unusual jewelry find and a memorable souvenir of your walking tour of Fairhope.

JM

Stowe's Jewelers
393 Fairhope Avenue

Founded in 1960 by Horace and Joy Stowe, Stowe's Jewelry is the second-oldest store on Fairhope Avenue. Beth Fugard and Peggy Williams, their daughters and the current proprietors, are proud to have celebrated sixty years in business.

Beth and Peggy assumed management of the store in 2007. They talked enthusiastically about the past and present of their enterprise, their variety of offerings, as well as their repair service.

They offer the only bridal registry in the area. Customers may sign up for sterling silverware. They specialize in custom design jewelry, and numerous local artists also bring their work to the store for sale.

It was surprising to see a large case devoted to gold-filled and sterling bangle bracelets which are in great demand. Featured also are the ever popular diamond and diamond stud earrings. Silver earrings are also available.

There is a right front wall display of costume jewelry, including a variety of bead necklaces fashioned from natural stones, including turquoise.

And that's not all! The case of watches contains the well-known brands, Bulova and Seiko. Be sure to see the beautiful antique jewelry items and antique watches.

When asked their primary specialty, Beth stated, "Customer service," a philosophy taught the sisters early by their parents.

Finally, Beth brought in a box covered in gossamer ribbons and topped with an unusual large shimmering bow. "Everybody knows us by our bows," she said.

JM

Wismar Jewelry
2 South Church Street

At his father's knee, Bill Wismar was intrigued by his father's profession as a jewelry maker/goldsmith, himself taught by old world trained German craftsmen. Soon Bill, still a young boy, was designing and making his own style of jewelry, much to his father's delight.

Today Bill strives to create wearable art with unique designs that's fun and exciting to wear. Bill says he makes his jewelry "heavy," so it can become a family heirloom to be handed down generation to generation. To accomplish this, Bill uses more gold or silver than in mass-produced jewelry, and he buys only the top triple-A gem stones available. In using this approach, Bill creates one-of-a-kind pieces not found anywhere else. All this and Bill keeps his prices reasonable because there is no middle man to take a big cut of the profits. Many visitors leave a drawing and choices of stones and receive their brooch, necklace, bracelet, or ring days later. Also found at his store are unique pieces created by award winning jewelry artisans located locally, regionally, or nationally.

Because Bill is also a highly regarded goldsmith, he can shorten, lengthen, or repair your existing jewelry, or use it to create something brand new and extraordinary. Want to surprise your wife on her birthday or anniversary? Talk to Bill; he has some ideas that will surprise you, and, more importantly, your wife.

RM

Lagniappe

There are More than Flies in Fly Creek

The denizens of Fly Creek include flies, of course. Also mosquitos, gnats (the horrible kind), fish, pelicans, the occasional osprey, a rare bald eagle, frogs, toads, turtles, snakes, and other sorts of water and mud dwelling creatures.

Two more notables of God's creatures that make their home down there from time to time are boat dwellers and alligators.

I spoke to one of them a couple of weeks ago. Seems that a large creature was living right over his den. "So, you didn't know that was a boat dweller's home?" I asked. He replied, "Of courssssssse, I didn't! How could I? I mean, that thing above my den you call a boat would move from time to time, and I guessed I figured there was some pretty big animal up there, but I had better things to worry about. It ain't an easy living these days, you know; you have to go out all the time and catch something or you jusssst go hungry!"

I looked him in his unblinking eye, and observed a piece of seaweed stuck in his terrible looking teeth, or was it seaweed? "Yeah, tell me about it. And the government doesn't make things any easier, either, do they? I mean, did you hear they are talking about dredging the creek?"

He opened his jaws a bit and hissed, a long drawn out sound of resignation, but with a hint of weary defiance. "I suppose they will expect me to move, but I am not going to. This is MY home, near MY family, and they have no right to evict me."

"But Leroy . . . you have not met Leroy, have you?" I asked. "He is the human who lives in the sailboat above your den."

"No," Mr. Gator said, "we've never been properly introduced."

"Well," I continued, "he was saying just the other day, wondering about what would happen if he slipped and fell off the dock into the mud and met one of your brothers."

Mr. Gator glared at me with a cold eye. "How would you like it if one of us gators came crashing through your living room ceiling one night and plopped down on your couch next to your wife or girlfriend while you were watching Alabama football and drinking beer? Of course, you would not be thrilled, right? No invitation, after all. No one could really blame you if you got excited. But us gators are not looking for trouble; we like peace and quiet, and a nice cool mud den. You don't bother us, and we'll try not to bother you. Fair, right?"

"Well, yeah, maybe . . . " I was somewhat embarrassed. Mr. Gator was a reasonable and respectable member of our community it seemed, despite the rumors I had heard. So I decided to be up front about things. "Mr. Gator, you know there are stories swirling about nefarious deeds late at night, dastardly doings attributed to you, things like missing cats and ducks. People are worried. Can you look at me and tell me with a straight face you have had nothing to do with any of those things?"

Mr. Gator's expression did not change one whit as he replied, "Of course, I had nothing to do with those things. Who are my accusers? Let me face them. Ducks! Cats! Ugh!" He made a disgusted hissing noise. Then he mumbled something about only a nut would think about cats with so many fish to concentrate on. "Why don't you go question the cat about what happened to the duck?" he asked.

"So, you are saying you would never entertain the thought of . . ."

"No, no, no," he interrupted before I could finish. "Fly Creek is a gator's gourmet paradise; why would I waste my time and palate on things like ducks? I never have, never will."

I gave him my best stern look. He did not appear intimidated, but I pressed on. "You are telling me you never, ever..." but I stopped as Mr. Gator suddenly thrashed his powerful tail, swirling the water so that the nearby sailboat pushed against its moorings. "NO!" he snorted. "Only if there is an irresistible temptation, which is very seldom, and besides, if a pig fell into your bedroom one night, you might thank the powers that be and have bacon for breakfast too!"

"I see," I replied, keeping a wary eye on the ever poised tail and noting the barely open jaws with their gnarly pointed rows of teeth. "Well, been nice talkin' to you. Gotta run now; see ya later." I turned and headed down the narrow pier.

"Yeah, sure, later," was all I heard him say over my shoulder. He sounded kinda blue.

A few days after that I was surprised to read an article in the local paper about a Labrador retriever that had survived an encounter with a large alligator while swimming in Fly Creek. It was reported that the gator backed down and swam away! But, now that Mr. Gator was officially "outed," his time was up. Sooner or later, another confrontation would follow, or an "irresistible temptation" would occur.

A nearby lake posts signs near swimming areas warning kids and dogs not to antagonize the alligators, but that is in a state park, not a public creek. In Fly Creek, large gators are not welcome. They just need to move on and find a different mud bank to make a den in.

With Mr. Gator gone now, Fly Creek feels a little lonely and somewhat less wild and natural. But hey....just wait a while, maybe next spring! KJ

Boutique Roundup

If you consider window shopping high art and one of your favorite pastime pleasures, then you are in for a pleasant experience while leisurely strolling our streets. Yes, we are a small town, but with a fashionable inclination. Who can resist stepping inside a store after some dazzling item of clothing in the display window has piqued your curiosity? Shopping can be a daunting task. So, we have attempted to give you an idea of what is out there and our humble method is to list the myriad of exciting name brands they offer. Good Luck. You can do it.

Adrenaline

328 Fairhope Avenue

Open 10 to 5 daily, Adrenaline offers hip, casual, cool men's and women's active wear. Brands include North Face, Patagonia, Rainbow, Olu Kai, Exofficio, Polar Bear, Coastal Cotton, Kavu, Kuhl, L-, Teva, Sanuk, and Ray Ban.

B Southern

314 De La Mare Suite A

Ladies, if you are going to live in the South, or visit here, you need to look the part. Tops and bottoms and everything in between, including shoes, jewelry, and sun glasses. Nice styles and nice selections. Current name brands include: Free People, Sundays, Sen, Sanctuary, Belladahl, Hippy Bird, Kinda Kist, and Middle End.

Cat's Meow

395 Fairhope Avenue

What can you say about a woman's clothing boutique that has a delicious 8,000 square feet of offerings? They do carry the largest collection of linen in town, along with great travel clothes and stylish yet comfortable shoes. And do not miss the dedicated back sales room with prices at fifty percent off and sometimes more. Stephanie stocks Miracle Body, Match Point, Fenini Renoir, Bunia, Dolma, Adrienne, Oddy, Hayden, Mittos, Ellison, Garcia, Brussola, Retrex, Corkus, and America Beyond.

CK Collections

320 Fairhope Avenue

Open 10 to 5 daily, this is our most sophisticated and most elaborate boutique. The store features the high end of the fashion world: Tom Ford, Lucky Star, Ciao Milano, Rag&Bone, Vince, Tory Burch, Chloe, Joie Dubarry, Este Lauder, Block Halo, Nicole Miller, and many more. Can be pricey. Big city attitude.

CK Collection Men's

306 De La Mare

Men, you will look like a million bucks in no time. GQ comes to Fairhope. Men's apparel from toe to top. Shoes, leather goods, pants, shirts, socks. Name brands include Barbour, Cole Haan, Agave, Billy Reid, Dubarry, Peter Miller, Beretta, and Southern Proper. George Clooney would shop here.

The Colony Shop
27 Section Street

Open 10 to 5 daily. Feminine Finery. Not exactly a boutique, but a well-stocked women's clothing store with pretty interesting styles. They obviously are in love with all things Johnny Was. But also Komaou XCVI, Lee Anderson, PJ Harlow, April Cornell, Luna Luz, Jane Yoo, GershonB RAM, Petite Tois, and Desiqual. Friendly salespeople wear what they sell.

Cybele's
382 Fairhope Avenue

Ladies fine clothing and accessories. 10 to 5 daily. Jean Clarkson stocks her shop with Joseph Ribkoff, Berek, Elliot Lauren, Planet, Simon Sebbag, Sharon Young, and more. She also carries a line of fine accessories.

East Bay Clothiers
39 North Section Street

Men's clothing with tons of style. A haberdashery for the sophisticated male. Great name brands, a great quality. Someone said Brad Pitt shops here. It's a rumor.

Four Bags
40 South Section Street

Sharon Davis loves interesting handcrafted and trendy hand bags from smallish boutique manufacturers. Some things are almost art, like her bamboo handbags from Cambodia. She also likes reasonable prices. And if it is raining, she carries a line of umbrellas that look like they were painted in the Louvre. Mona B, Pouchee, and others. There is handcrafted jewelry and a great collection of scarves—and orange slices are free.

The Fairhope Store
323 De la Mare

Long-time resident Lisette Norman takes pride in her hometown with a store that pays homage to all things Fairhope. Looking to show where you have been? Then a shirt emblazoned with the famous pier and name "Fairhope" is just right for you. Beach umbrellas, towels? Same goes for them. T-shirts, sweat shirts, beach wear. A great place to start your shopping.

GiGi & Jay's
400 Fairhope Avenue

Yes, we will call this a boutique, but it is for children, youth, and infants. Maybe we should call it a kidtique. With upbeat and upscale clothing and gifts, this is the place to go for a baby shower gift. They offer Johnnie-O, Kissy Kissy, Aftco, Splendid, Ella Moss, Florence Eisman, Little English, Bailey Boys, Southern Tide.

LaRobe
318 A Fairhope Avenue

10 to 5 daily. Twenty or so brands. Quality oriented women's clothing for the pizzazz niche market.

Le Papillion
319 Fairhope Avenue

Linda decided her boutique would be a mixture of gifts, art, and fashion apparel for women. It is tucked away on Fairhope Avenue with an interesting side entrance. You will find Ganz, Ungee, Charley Page, and lots of others. She features local handmade jewelry.

The Little Drawer
309 De la Mare

A fascinating lingerie boutique. Faith Miller chooses upscale little things for the young woman. Eberjey, Hanky Panky, Chantelle, Simone Perele, Natori, Spanx, LeGent, Naked Business. Bedhead. Personalized Bra fittings. Upscale/quality.

M&F Casuals
380 Fairhope Avenue

Open 9:30 to 5:30 daily. Casual clothing for a casual lifestyle. Lisette, Comfy USA, Sympli, Oh My Gauze, Flax, Brighton, Foxcroft, Simply Southern.

Ooh La La
225 Fairhope Avenue

Tracey Macaro offers her own name brand. Exclusive styles with a Paris perspective. Eiffel Designs. Some jewelry, allergy free. Trendy and smart.

Private Gallery
310 Fairhope Avenue

Interesting in that the store is the site of the old Gulf Gas Station of 1930. Stocked with affordable and trendy things. Umgee, Everly, Entro, Grace Yingling, Zen, Lollipop, Piko. Ellison, Mittoshop. Designer Jewelry by Philippe.

Rush
58 S. South Section

Another new shop to grace South Section Street is Rush, and while small in square footage, Jennifer fills it nicely with leading style apparel for young women and at exceptional prices. Brands include Mustard Seed, Wish List, Do+Be, and more. She also carries shoes and several lines of jewelry.

7 South
7 South Section Street

Beth and Jody decided they wanted to open a men's and women's apparel store with an upscale air about it. One of the few in Fairhope to stock both. Highlighted brands include On Running, Hard Tail, Able, Onward Reserve, AFTCO, ALO, and Old Point Clear.

Sadie's
5 South Section Street

Mary Knox Mundy calls her little hideaway a contemporary style women's boutique. She packs the place with Tina Turk,

JBrand, Alice and Trixie, BCBG, Splendid, Wildfox, Lavender Brain, and Bishop+Young.

Shoefly

326 Fairhope Avenue

10 to 5 daily. A shoe store for shoe fanatics. Hobo International, All Black, Korkease, Seychelles, Latigo, B.C., Hobo, Chocolate Blu, OTBT, Doce Vita, Miz Modz, Chaco, Antelope, Coconuts, and much more.

Southern Gents

314 De La Mare Suite C

It is nice to have a new men's clothing store in town and if you have the eye for the finer things in life, this may be the place for you. They carry shirts, shorts, pants, shoes, ties, underwear, and leather goods. Pricey but excellent quality.

Stephanie Downtown

14 South Section Street

Cathy and Stephanie cater to women of all ages, carrying exclusive brands tilting toward the upscale. Nouvelle, Palm Beach, Gracia, Tractr, Kaeli Smith, Joy Joy, Gabby Isabella, and Coobie can be found in this former law office turned stylish boutique.

Sway

324 Fairhope Avenue

A hip woman's boutique for everyday needs. Berkley Delaney stocks her shop with Free People, Seafolly, Bobeau, Kut By The Cloth, Sisters, Parker Smith, Blue Life, Helen John, and more.

Tiny Town

337 Fairhope Avenue

Shouldn't young, well behaved and adored children have their own boutique? Holly thinks so, and she exemplifies her thinking with a fun and color-filled store. She carries a mixture of things for the new born to age fourteen youngsters. You will find apparel, books, toys, and heirloom items. If you are a mom or grandmother and want your prodigy to look their best, you have found a home. Do not overlook the Noodle & Boo lotions.

Utopia
318 B Fairhope Avenue

Barbra Ladnier brings to Fairhope Umgee, Entro, Elan, Honey Me, BW Pepper, Charcoal, and more. She says she loves casual, friendly, everyday, trendy, and affordable clothing. 10 to 5 daily.

Vine
412 Fairhope Avenue

Tucked into a little spot so tight we had to inhale to get in, Vine is a trendy boutique with a big local following. Unique styles, affordable for the younger set, include Mink Pink, On the Road Amuse Society, Some Days Lovin', Pistola, Gentle Fawn, Project Social-T, Amuse, 15-30, and Kerisma.

Roundup by RM

Lagniappe

Wildlife

Because Fairhope is situated near the bay with nearby marshlands and thick woods, we have some friends who live near us and many have four feet.

I will start with the largest. Yes, we have a few alligators around here. Most of our green friends lazily travel up and down the bay, and a few drop off their youngsters in the bayous and inlets to snack and grow a little larger before rejoining their parents upstream. The larger specimens usually travel up to the headwaters at Five Rivers. Some will approach eight to ten feet long. They rarely come onto our beaches and normally swim hundreds of feet off shore

Fairhope is also home to lazy foxes, raccoons, armadillos, turtles, and possum. Deer are rare in downtown Fairhope because somebody would probably shoot them. But a few pop up now and then — usually near golf courses.

In the flying category, we pride ourselves on pelicans that easily circle over Fairhope day in and day out. There are also colonies of bats that come out toward the evening and are misidentified as swallows by most. They casually swoop over Fairhope nightly, dining on night flying insects. Yes, hallelujah, they eat mosquitos.

Also at evening time, and because of our heavy rainfall and expanse of woods nearby, we have assemblies of many choruses made up of petite green tree frogs. Assemblies does not properly describe the exact numbers. Some say hundreds of thousands, I say millions. If you are not acquainted, I will describe one. It is the size of a quarter, an enchanting green color, and they can stick to anything smooth with their little suction cup toes. About nightfall they awaken from their day-long nap and start their singing. Some have called it a "din," but I disagree. I had one or two jump from a branch and land on my shirt and even my face. I was charmed by the visitor. He or she stayed there for a few minutes thinking about the situation, then jumped into a nearby shrub. They truly believe we humans are trees that can walk.

One last thing, a fair amount of outside cats live among us. You will find those sleeping on porch roofs or car roofs in the winter, and under porches, cars, or magnolia trees in the summer. Go ahead and talk to them if you desire. Just squat down to their level and say slowly in a true Alabama, Mississippi, or Georgia accent, "Good mornin', how y'all doin'? Y'all doin' OK?"

But be forewarned, we have the certifiably laziest cats east of the Mississippi. Some will open one eye and look you over. Others might open two eyes. And if one gets up, meows and walks down to where you are squatting, then that is not a true Fairhope cat. That is a newcomer and does not yet know the Fairhope cat rules.

And that, dear friends, is the list of wild life here in Fairhope. Lazy alligators, lazy armadillos, lazy foxes, lazy possums, lazy pelicans, lazy tree frogs, and last but not least lazy cats.

As my friend Milliard Delmore has said many times sitting on his front porch swing sipping his sweet tea, "I swear there is something in our water. It causes laziness."

Yes, there is. There sure is.

RM

Consignment

Back on the Rack
407 Fairhope Avenue

Back on the Rack is an upscale consignment boutique where shoppers can browse for designer clothing, handbags, jewelry, and shoes, hoping to score an expensive, designer look for a fraction of the original cost. Depending on current inventory, a selection of sunglasses and designer luggage is also available. As with all consignment shops, the inventory depends on a steady flow of women bringing in their clean, current, name brand items.

Clothing items are neatly displayed by size and color on racks for trousers, tops, and dresses.

The shop was buzzing with customers when this writer visited, but I was told there are lines for the dressing rooms during prom and Mardi Gras season.

It's worth a look to see if you can go home with a like-new designer item to enhance your wardrobe. You never know what you might find.

RG

Hertha's Second Edition
330 Fairhope Avenue

She is the Coco Chanel, the unique, creative couturier of downtown Fairhope, channeling new and vintage garments, jewelry, hats, scarves, wraps, coats, shoes, and gloves of every color and size.

You will be welcomed and assisted in this world of upscale consignment fashion.

Hertha's daughter, Lurleen Fuller, is the present owner, who, following the philosophy of her mother, the trailblazer of consignment shopping, stresses the finer points of quality and authenticity in brand offerings. What continues to drive her, she says, "are the rewards from customers who thank her for helping them to feel good about their clothes."

You will appreciate the twenty-five to seventy-five percent discounts on everything, including genuine and faux furs, guaranteed to be in style.

Consignments are acquired from those having changed sizes since last season, recently changed hair color, suggesting a new wardrobe, or perhaps having a desire to swap a fashion trend for a retro style regularly on display in the shop.

Hertha's is fairy godmother to superannuated ladies on Social Security, as well as Cinderellas on a budget who mimic the tastes of oil magnates' wives who frequent Neiman Marcus. They happily hand over a modicum of cash for a frock or slippers fit for a princess, and have enough left over for a supper of fried chicken, okra, and homegrown tomatoes.

Hertha's is a rescue haven for those who grieve for a dress, blouse, or scarf given away in haste and who later continue an on-going search for a replacement.

A tour of the shop surprises the shopper with designs of Art Deco reminiscent of the halls of Tutankhamun or the boudoirs of desert princes. Continuing through the shop, one discovers silver, gold lamé, and lace wraps.

Hertha's is the place to purchase a wide variety of garments for an equally wide variety of occasions: a glitzy wrap for Mardi Gras or a silk ensemble for a mother of the bride. The patron—whether size four or twenty-four, age eighteen or eighty—will leave elated over her selections, feeling glamorous, and, looking in the mirror, she will see a full-length reflection of Cindy Crawford.

Two young professional women, one a surgeon from Baltimore and the other a sales executive from Denver, made their annual visit to their aunt in Fairhope. The second day of their visit was usually a shopping trip to Hertha's Second Edition consignment shop.

They said their current need was jewelry suited to their petite sizes and personalities, as well as to some new garments recently purchased. They had been discouraged recently to find only oversized jewelry which they said felt overwhelming. They were now delighted to find the size and style they were looking for: a tiny shimmering chain with a 13-millimeter pearl in the center. The brand is called "Make A Wish," the creation of a New York designer.

The women purchased several different styles, and told their aunt how excited they were to find "exactly what they were wishing for—the name fit."

The aunt was happy in the assurance her nieces had an extra incentive for a return visit to Fairhope in the near future.

JM

Revolution Resale
9 North Church Street

Fashions and accessories with a youthful appeal are on the racks at Revolution Resale.

The younger vibe is apparent when entering the shop, which is larger than it seems from the outside. Different from other consignment resale shops in the area, men's clothing is also on the racks. For the prom or Mardi Gras ball goers, you'll find an amazing and sparkling back room full of ball gowns.

The shop is worth a browse for the young and young-at-heart.

RG

Art Galleries

Eastern Shore Art Center
401 Oak Street (just off Fairhope Avenue)

Perhaps no place in Fairhope better exemplifies the vibrant, creative spirit that lives here than the Eastern Shore Art Center. Part gallery, part museum, this local treasure is the beating heart of the visual arts scene. It has been the gathering place for painters, sculptors, ceramicists, and photographers for the fifty-four years of its existence.

In each of its six gallery spaces can be found worthwhile exhibits featuring not only work of local artists, but numerous out of towners, as well as shows with a national scope. One of the highlights each year is the National Watercolor Society traveling exhibit featuring award winning work by artists from all over the world. The exhibits change monthly—just check the website: *esartcenter.org*. Also, throughout the year ESAC offers an appealing selection of classes and workshops taught by practicing professionals.

And if you are looking for a one-of-a-kind gift, please step inside the unusual and exciting gift shop. There you will find affordable jewelry, books, ceramics, hand-made scarves, and original artwork, all of which you will see nowhere else.

If your time in Fairhope happens to coincide with the first Friday of the month between six and eight p.m., do not miss the First Friday Artwalk. The Eastern Shore Art Center is the place to begin this fun downtown happening. The Art Center is open Tuesday-Saturday, and is free to the public.

EG

Fairhope Artist Gallery
18 South Section Street

Here you will find artists who are making a living at being artists. It is a co-op of sorts, and the walls are covered with lots of local talent and atmosphere. Prices are quite reasonable, and you can walk out with a nice work that just might become a sought after treasure your children all hope to inherit. Gigi Hackford is the dynamo behind the scenes and has become quite a treasure for the people of Fairhope. David Tate is another of our up and coming painters whose works are now hanging on walls in most of the south. The FAG represents about thirty artists, whose styles and technique are on full display. You can get lost in this place.

RM

Gallery by the Bay
386 Fairhope Avenue

Seeley's Gallery by the Bay features the work of more than twenty local artists, some of whom show internationally. Their Fairhope exhibits are exclusively at Gallery by the Bay, however.

Among the works gracing Seeley's walls are pieces by Linson, Oxford, McKee, Westerberg, and many more. The Gallery offers original oils, water colors, acrylics, giclees, designer jewelry, pottery, glass, wood turning, photography, sculpture, leather, The Fairhope Christmas Card, Fairhope notecards, puzzles, and ornaments, plus much more.

Each First Friday Art Walk, the Gallery features one artist, and they have an annual benefit show as well. Seeley will ship for out-of-town buyers.

Open 10-5 Monday through Saturday.

PP

The Kiln Studio & Gallery
9 North Church Street

For readers interested in pottery artwork, Fairhope has just the place for you: *The Kiln Studio & Gallery.* You will find ceramic art, created by local and regional artists, for sale in the gallery. In the studio, you may pursue your passion for creating pottery artwork, thereby furthering the enjoyment of your Fairhope experience. Susie Bowman, a well-known artist and a Fairhope resident, established the Kiln in 2010. Her love of the pottery art form will be obvious to you at your first meeting.

Susie offers workshops in the studio, ranging in length from a three-hour afternoon session to several weeks. Clay, firing, and glazing are included. The studio has pottery wheels and two kilns. Susie and her store manager will be there to assist you. Some workshops are conducted by visiting internationally well-known artists, such as Ron Meyers, professor emeritus at the University of Georgia. Members of The Kiln create pottery art in the studio on a regular basis.

In the gallery, Susie leans toward displays of creations by local artists and well-known artists like Meyers. Shipping arrangements are available.

Susie tells that after her children were grown, she decided to return to the work world and pursue her passion for all things pottery. She said she believes the most elemental connection to our earth is working in clay. "It is an essential need for any potter to feel this association to their world," she said. "Working with clay provides space and rhythm, while constantly challenging and teaching me as I work."

She sought advice from Meyers at the beginning of her dream to open The Kiln, because he was so prominently known in the field of ceramics. She had only met him briefly at the University of Georgia. Would he remember her? Yes, he did, and he came to her aid. Susie said she is thankful to Ron and the many other artists who have helped her pursue her dream.

This writer witnessed the ongoing creative activity and the beautiful artwork displayed at the Kiln and encourages you to check it out. If you are an out-of-town visitor, take this book home with you and show it to your pottery fan friends back there. They can reach Susie at 251-517-5460 or thekilnstudio@yahoo.com. The web site is www.thekilnstudio.com.

JW

Lyons Share Gallery
330 De La Mare

Mike Lyons is a force of nature and already a legend up and down De la Mare. For example, there is always something exciting happening at his Lyons Share Gallery and he is always at the center of it.

Besides the stuffed goat that resides upstairs or down, and besides the custom frames he produces using one-hundred-year-old recycled Cypress beaded board, there is always the art. Fresh, inventive, and outstanding pieces from the region's best artists can be found here. There is lots to see in the main gallery or the small side gallery behind the glass garage door, but please climb the long and wide stair case to the second floor gallery to see some wonderful pieces at affordable prices.

It is noteworthy that Mike and Kelly represent artists that are on display in the best art galleries in Atlanta and New Orleans. If you are fortunate enough to be here on First Friday Art Walk night, this is the place to start as some of the showings sell out within hours. And oh yes. It is the best frame shop around.

RM

Nall Gallery/Studio
414 Equality Avenue

He is famous in France and Italy, and he is famous here. Nall is loved by many and always entertaining. You may notice his style is unique, which is why no one is trying to replicate him.

When in town, Nall is sometimes welcoming guests to his one-of-a-kind gallery/studio. Just tap at the glass door and, if the stars are aligned for you and he needs a break, he may invite you in for a short guided tour. If he is busy, he will just wave back with a nice smile. Which means you can just stand outside his window and watch him work.

Many of his creations can be admired from inches away, but if you are staying at the Grand Hotel, the lobby is a showcase of Nall's creations for you to admire close up. Nall exhibits no other works than his own; this is, after all, his one and only studio. And he is Nall.

RM

Lagniappe

The Flowers in Fairhope

Fairhope has not always flourished with colorful flowers. While plants grow well in this sub-tropical climate, the founders of the town arrived with economics, not flowers, on their minds. Matter of fact, in order to build the Utopia envisioned on the drawing board, the dense forest within the founding Single Tax Colony property was totally cut for homes and business construction. By 1920, the trees were gone and the land laid barren of trees. Only bushes and some plants around homes remained. This caused significant erosion of the land, but that's another story.

The new town prospered as a resort destination in spite of its bland appearance, due to the sandy beaches, sea breezes, and the absence of Yellow Fever that threatened residents over in Mobile. The error of deforestation was realized and replanting of trees began, mostly with nature taking the lead. When the Causeway opened in 1927, business and shop sales on the Eastern Shore dropped off, as residents could more easily access stores in Mobile. Several ideas were implemented to regain visitors and souvenir buyers. In the 1950s, the Arts and Crafts Festival began. In the 1970s, Mayor Jim Nix initiated a beautification program. After becoming mayor, he and his family traveled to Europe and were impressed by the beauty and therapy of flowers in the towns and villages. He said, "We can do that," and when he returned to Fairhope, he and the City Council created a horticulture program and emphasized flowers to draw tourists.

The city now has flowers on downtown street corners, in over a hundred hanging baskets, in eighty flower boxes, and on about fifty wooden trash bin tops. The flowers are exchanged four-times a year with mature already-blooming color of the seasons. Caladiums, petunias, tulips, gladiolus, paper-whites, and annuals

Photo by Robert Glennon

decorate everywhere. Baskets of flowers, watered daily, hang from lampposts throughout downtown. The beautiful flora and the annual Arts and Crafts Festival each March attract thousands. And in late November, the flowers are accented by the lighting of the downtown trees, which provide a festive spirit throughout the holiday season. In 2002, Fairhope received the  National America in Bloom Award for its flowers. The program has now expanded to include large flowerbeds on Greeno Road / Highway 98 and Shumard Oak trees in medians on Fairhope Avenue and Greeno Road.

The rose garden was also added at the Fairhope Pier. Tons of dirt were deposited to reclaim the shoreline, and seawalls were constructed to protect against erosion in the gullies. Over one thousand rose bushes and forty-one varieties of roses are in the garden. They are pruned, weeded, and sprayed each week during the spring and summer, and the grass is mowed three times a week. The National All-America Rose Selections organization has recognized Fairhope twice over the years for its roses and commitment to landscaping. The rose garden area now draws hundreds of people on summer evenings to see the color and amazing sunsets. The flowers have stimulated the economy!

RMG

Interior Design

Copper Column
311 De la Mare

Let's take a little walk back in time, shall we? This gift shop and gallery is a lot of things. But most of all, it is an adventure.

From the street, it looks like it could be a bar and hangout where nefarious citizens gather to drink and plan questionable deeds. It is not. Wander past the court yard and past the corrugated tin façade and into a world of esoteric items to decorate your home.

Lamps, art, fabric, signs, candles. Suzanne Davis stocks her studio with a twinkle in her eye, and an eye for style. There are three, maybe four, rooms all loaded with one-of-a-kind objects. And as our deadline approaches, she tells me she is opening a bar in the back. Live music to follow. A fun place to venture with a glass of chilled chardonnay in hand.

RM

Green Gates Downtown
150 North Section Street.

Please hold your oohs and aahs when you walk into Green Gates, or someone will think you have never seen fabulous beach decor before. First and foremost, this is casual elegance perfect for any home near the water. Everything, and we mean everything, has a salt water quality about it. Standing by a sofa, I could almost hear Gulf breezes as they push blue-green waves crashing into the beach. What we are saying is somehow there is a built in fragrance of sun tan oil and salt water. Everything is well thought out, and precisely and wonderfully executed.

Rene Mashburn is the owner and the lady who has the eye for detail, quality, and craftsmanship. We noticed a group of ladies from out of town who were talking about how to get this or that into their car and back to Atlanta. Good luck, girls.

So now that we have your attention, here is what they offer. Incredible chairs and sofas, rugs, parsons tables, more incredible chairs and sofas, lamps, pillows, paintings by local artists, and ceramics of all shapes and sizes. We also observed quite a collection of jewelry and fabrics for all things dining. I imagined those ladies from Atlanta spent a good hour and a half there and left with an arm load of prizes headed toward Georgia.

Some of the name brands we saw were Dovetail, Arteriors, Bliss Studio, Sarreid, Regin/Andrew, Fortunata, Gabby, Guild Masters, Aidan Gray, Four Hands, Emissary, and Lacefield Design. Obviously, there are more. You just have to ask. And yes, things are a little pricey, but then if you're not worth it, who is? Open 10 to 5 Daily.

RM

Objects
25 B South Section Street

This store, a staple for Fairhope home decorators, has wonderful items waiting here for you and us. And these interesting, never-in-normal-stores items are waiting to be taken home, not only for your home but for your personal use. Things like candles, lotions, jewelry, and perfumes. And serious decorating and occasional pieces like sofas, tables, chairs, rugs, pillows, and paintings.

Name brands you will see are Vera Bradley, Scout, Thymes, Pursen, Corkcicle, Happy Everything, Tervis, Coffee Bean, Beach days, Mersea, Hobo, Spartina 449, Beatrice Ball, Vetiver, and Trapp. Yes, as my friend says, Lynn Boothe and Kimberley Lang have upped the ante here. The last thing we wanted to say is the best thing about the store is that they change their offerings so often that a month from now, they may have a whole group of new things to show you.

RM

Vellum and Velvet
404 Fairhope Avenue

This store is where my friends who read *Architectural Digest* and *Veranda* come to gather those items that set them apart. This design store has the ultimate fabrics for pillows or drapes or whatever you want to cover. Savannah does not stop there, as she carries a tasteful line of lamps, sofas, wall paper, and one-of-a-kind designer items. Always inspiring.

RM

Villa Décor

306 Fairhope Avenue

This is one of our favorite stores in Fairhope because it makes us feel that we just stepped into the pages of *Architectural Digest*. Let's begin with chandeliers. They have possibly one of the largest collections we've seen, with a range of styles to suit you, me, and my mother-in-law. Large to small, brass to wood, crystal to bronze. Any one of these designs will make your dining room or entryway come alive with floating, elegant style. These chandeliers greet your visitors with something overhead to dazzle the senses.

Wait a minute; look down at the floor and gaze at a delicious array of Oushak rugs. Most are done by hand, either hand knotted or hand loomed. Some are small for accent areas or some are large to fill your bedroom in muted old world colors that soften any room. And how about a sophisticated dining table made of fine white porcelain and concrete? Sounds strange, but it is all in the execution. Occasional lamps on your "I need to get" list? Some of these gems will be the focus of any room you put them in. And, of course, we all have to sit down and rest while in our confusion as what to buy next. So choose from a wonderful assortment of chairs, chaise lounges, or a stylish sofa.

The owner also has an eye for fine ceramics, including a one-of-a-kind collection of handmade bowls decorated with delicate white rose blossoms. We particularly liked a shallow bowl perfect for floating your own white or pink or yellow rose blossoms. As you can tell, we are thrilled such a store is in our little village. It means we don't have to drive to Dallas or Atlanta to find such stylish pieces. Take your time here and don't miss that one-of-a-kind gem hiding behind a delightful vase near that exquisite floor lamp. Open 10 to 5 daily.

RM

Antiques

Betty G. Haynie Antiques & Fine Art
15 N. Section Street

Truly fine English, American, and French antiques are on the display floor at Betty Haynie Antiques and Fine Art. Ms. Haynie has been in the antique business for decades, and her shop is known for museum quality furniture, accessories, rugs, artwork, mirrors, and glassware. You will also find elegant silver and silver plate, Spode china, Majolica, Imari, Chinese export, English ironstone, and Staffordshire.

Most items are obtained from estate sales near and far, and the web site is always full of beautiful offerings in all of the above categories. Nothing beats a stroll around the shop, though, for a peek into past elegance. Appraisal services are also available.

Oh…if you wish to make a purchase and the item won't fit into your back seat or your minivan, items can be expertly packed and shipped for you.

Be sure and stroll through this fine shop for another one of your Fairhope experiences. The shop is open during the monthly First Friday Art Walk, so stop in then for some wine.

RG

Copper Roof Antiques
416 Fairhope Avenue

The first time I wandered into Copper Roof Antiques, I was impressed by their selection of everyday "practical" antiques. Things such as clocks, crystal, china, porcelain, silver, small furniture, kitchenware, knick knacks, hand tools, and other items that could find a good use in the house as well as being much better quality than discount store items and having timeless classic looks.

I spied a pretty French made solid brass 1950-ish small alarm clock, and a humongous, serious looking, very old, one-man tree saw. I wanted both, but didn't have enough cash on hand. So, I came back the next week.

That day, a Tuesday, Edda and Eric Gilbert, who jointly were one of the fourteen booth owners at the shop, were presiding. Eric regaled me with history and stories of his native London, England, while Edda took care of ringing up my purchases and wrapping them.

I went there again a few days later and met Mrs. Carolyn Davis, another booth owner who was tending the shop that day. I found a wonderful purple glass doorknob and a nice bone handled knife. Maybe I will pick them up next time.

For economically priced practical treasures, this place can't be beat.

They are open from ten-ish in the morning to about five in the afternoon, Monday through Friday. Stop by and spend some time.

KJ

Crown & Colony Antiques
24 South Section Street

Let's say you are looking for a single French antique, say a Trumeau mirror, 1870 to 1900. And it would really set off your dining room to rival your best friend Suzie's dining room and you don't know where to look and you don't want to travel to France to find one. Darling, we have just the place for you. Crown & Colony has been collecting such wonders since 1992.

They travel every two months to France, Italy, Britain, and Belgium to gather a shipping container of such wonderful things and then put them on display in their large showrooms. The proprietors and taste makers here are Peter and Ann Fargason, and Ann has quite an eye for one-of-a-kind, quality antiques that you will usually only find at the finest salons in New York, Boston, Dallas, or Atlanta. I particularly had my eye on an Italian chandelier, two armoires, three bonnetieres, and a graceful buffet deux corps.

If you don't have time to stop in, go to their web site and they will present to you their current collection. They have two other locations here in Fairhope for specialized antiques, and both are within walking distance. If you are from out of town, they will ship for you.

RM

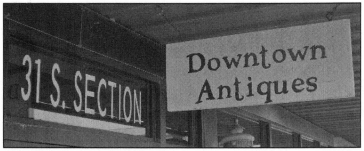

Downtown Antiques

31 S. Section Street

Michele Craft, owner and manager of Downtown Antiques, has seen many changes since she opened the shop on Section Street over a decade ago. New homes were larger, purse strings were looser, and almost every shopper was either collecting something or shopping for a gift for someone else who collected something back in the days before the economic downturn.

Downtown Antiques' aisles are wide; and the displays are light, bright, and orderly. The usual dark furniture and accessories do not take center stage here. Many of Michele's customers are seeking a look that reflects the warm and sunny beach climate.

There are many handmade pillows scattered throughout the shop. Collectibles, such as a display of antique perfume bottles, are displayed in groups. There are many side tables, dining tables, chairs, curio cabinets, headboards, and dressers. A small niche offers a selection of vintage clothing. Youngsters can check out the shelves of classic children's books.

Many of the furniture items have had the benefit of Michele's magic touch with a paint brush. She can brighten up a dreary table or distress a cabinet that has seen better days, creating a whole new look. The shop is open six days a week, so Michele has to confine her "craft-y" skills to Sundays.

Items are priced well and would be a nice keepsake of a trip to downtown Fairhope. Drop in and see.

RG

R. F. Architectural & Garden Antiques
61 S. Church Street

Pass through the tall, metal gates at Architectural & Garden Antiques and you will feel as though you were entering an olive harvest in the French or Tuscan countryside. Huge clay olive jars fill the outdoor space, some more than four feet tall. Concrete planters, lintels, statuary, and balustrades are scattered throughout the entry yard. Tall pine trees shade the yard, making browsing a cool and pleasant experience. The rustic interior of the building is streaked with afternoon sunlight as I enter. I hear the sound of creaking wood floors and inhale the scent of antiquities. I see a stack of old books topped by an antique magnifying glass; a deer-hoof gun rack; antique light fixtures overhead; and tall armoires, sideboards, and chests line the batten walls. Sconces, church relics, statues of saints and popes, and centuries-old paintings are placed in every niche. Chipped wooden statues of Mary and Joseph look at me with supplicating eyes, perhaps beseeching me to take them home with me. I can't help but wish I knew the stories of many of these items—where they came from and the journey they have been on for the past centuries.

This location is one of three galleries owned and operated by the Fargason family. The other locations are Crown and Colony Antiques on Section Street, and Aubergine Culinary Antiques and Oriental Rugs on De la Mare Street.

The owners make frequent trips to Italy, Germany, Belgium, England, and France, searching for antiques and decorative accessories, normally receiving a new shipment every month. Inventory turns over frequently. Prices are competitive, and the shop has an online presence, making it easy to search for specific items.

Architectural & Garden Antiques is a trip into another world beyond the usual tourist fare. A browser's delight.

RG

Toys, Books and More

The Book Inn

15 S. Section Street

Passing through the front door of The Book Inn, a used book store, customers are greeted by an aroma somewhere between "book store" and "library." Any avid reader knows this fragrance and it triggers an immediate urge to explore the stacks of books that line the shelves in every direction. In an unusual arrangement, the books are stacked pancake style, on their sides. This enables the browser to see the titles and authors without bending sideways to read the spine of the book. There are thousands of books on the shelves in a large number of genres. They are clearly stacked under signs identifying them by genre and author, making it simple to find whatever the customer is looking for.

The Book Inn has occupied the storefront on Section Street for thirty-eight years. The current owner, Coleen Avritt, began working at the used book store twenty-eight years ago, and when her former boss was ready to sell a few years ago, she bought the business. She enjoys her work and loves to share her love of books with the many tourists and locals who drop in to her store.

Books are traded two for one, plus local tax and a small service charge. A card file contains the names and trade information for hundreds of customers so they can come to redeem their trade points at their convenience. Walk-ins who are not traders can purchase books for forty percent off the cover price.

Regular traders walk through the door with a few or a bundle or bag full of books to trade. Coleen and her small staff sort through the books, organizing them by genre. Occasionally books can be rejected if they are inappropriate for the Fairhope market or if there are too many of a particular title.

Customers enjoy the fun of finding things they haven't been able to locate anywhere else. Current titles share the shelf space with old favorites no longer on the shelf at the regular book store. Hard and soft cover books, as well as audio books, are available.

Come in, cool off, browse, and enjoy the extraordinary inventory at The Book Inn.

RG

Bouch's Premium Cigars and Accessories
77 South Section Street

Cigar enthusiasts, Fairhope has you covered. Even the local Piggly Wiggly has a humidor in the wine department filled with a variety of respectable cigars.

If you are a true dyed-in-the-wool cigar aficionado, you will want to take in Bouch's Premium Cigars. With more than 350 different cigars to choose from, the most discriminating smoker will find something special.

Bouch's also carries humidors, cases, cutters, and lighters. If you don't want to smoke alone, most afternoons find a gathering of like-minded cigar appreciators relaxing, talking, and enjoying a fine cigar in the front parlor of the shop.

PP

Doctor Music
35 South Section Street

The mad man who owns this store loves all things old and he loves all things music. This is probably why he scours every thrift shop and garage sale for real old luggage. Let's say a 1948 American Tourister, the type you see in those Humphrey Bogart,

Veronica Lake movies. Sometimes made of real leather and in great shape. Then Doctor Music, who also is known as Wade Wellborn, takes them back to his secret shop located somewhere hidden in Fairhope and packs two six-inch, very sensitive stereo woofers and tweeters and an amplifier inside, punches some holes in the case, then adds a connector so you can play your iPhone or iPod with incredible clarity and fidelity. All of this magic fidelity comes out of what appears to be a wonderful vintage suitcase. But to most people hearing it for the first time, you will hear them say, "Where is that divine music coming from?" Most will never think it is coming from that handsome vintage two-tone Samsonite suitcase sitting in the corner. Yes, it's old; yes, it's art; and yes, it adds a sense of style to your living room or den. Some people have seen them on TV and ordered them from as far away as San Francisco or New York City.

But that is just the beginning of visiting Dr. Music's store on Section Street. What else will you find there? CDs by the thousands. LPs by the thousands. And now, even brand new high-end record players. Yes, turntables are back. But let's say you are looking for an Everly Brothers greatest hit LP. Wade has it. Aretha Franklin? Yep. And Johnny Cash, Alabama, Frank Sinatra, and The Clash. Some rare, some not so rare. And not just used, but new, still in the wrapper, and for a good price. You see, Dr. Music has a following. They watch what is in the store, the real store and the EBay store, and get first dibs. Dr. Music is more than a record store—as we used to call them—Dr. Music is all things music.

One thing more, there is a persistent rumor that once upon a time in 1969 Roy Orbison visited Fairhope and liked it so much that after he died, he came back to hang out at Dr. Music's—sort of spirit wise that is—and about three in the morning, neighbors say, you might hear Roy singing "Only the Lonely," accompanied by a single guitar. Sometimes with a solo piano, or if you are lucky, you may hear "Blue Bayou." There have been discussions about this phenomenon at the local coffee shop across the street. I have my doubts, because it could just be Dr. Music trying out a new cross-over circuit board for his latest speakers in a 1954 Amelia Earhart brown and tan suitcase. Either way, it is a great place to kill some time and listen to some great music, and, who knows, maybe Roy will tap you on your shoulder and point out his favorite Johnny Cash LP.

RM

Fairhope Pharmacy
398 Fairhope Avenue

Fairhope Pharmacy, an historic landmark in downtown Fairhope, has its origin in the early 1900s, when Dr. Clarence L. Mershon, one of the founders of the Single Tax Colony, practiced medicine in his office and dispensed drugs there. In 1916, he built the drug store. In 1957, Ben Barnhill joined as the pharmacist. He bought the store in 1959.

Originally, it contained a soda fountain with attached stools. This was replaced later by walls and standing shelves and first aid items. Prescriptions acquired in the pharmacy are filled based on the local physicians' orders and occasional special orders based on customers' needs. It is the only independent drug store on the Eastern Shore and the only one in the city that makes deliveries.

Gradually, cosmetics, exclusive designer perfumes, and other personal items began to take over much of the front area space. In 2001, Mrs. Barnhill and their daughter, Lou Anne Harrell, suggested adding artistic and seasonal displays be placed in the front windows. This led to the many gift items abundantly offered throughout the store. Colorful designer articles in china, pottery, ceramics, glassware, and hand-painted and printed pillows give the appearance of an art gallery. All kinds of personal accessories, such as designer eyeglasses and umbrellas, fill the shelves. Jewelry is abundant in every form and type—bracelets, rings, and necklaces invite the customer to try them on. Figurines beckon from the high shelves. The most popular items in the store are pillows, some of which highlight the favorite sea birds and Fairhope mementos. These greet customers at the front door.

Not to be outdone by the boutiques and gift shops, Fairhope Pharmacy contains lacy and crocheted tops, wraps, and cover-ups in bright colors and designs hanging from the shelves. Tourists and local customers who make a quick stop at the store for an over-the-counter item are sure to be waylaid by the gallery-like atmosphere and the profusion of assorted gift items and the opportunity to take home a special treat.

Fairhope Pharmacy never fails to surprise and delight with its continual additions of unusual, stylish apparel, such as shawls, tops, purses, and elegant wraps. Lou Anne Harrell was eager to say more clothing lines have been added, as well as devotional books, and little gifts such as magnets, key rings, and jewelry. Post cards featuring Fairhope scenes and motifs are a favorite.

The Pharmacy is upping its claim as a competitor to the apparel stores. A new feature is stylish rain boots.

A new pottery collection exhibits the artistry of potter Randolf Pryor and his coastal motifs of crabs and fish.

A customer's trip to Fairhope Pharmacy for drug and health items will surely be interrupted by the new array of apparel, pottery, and Fairhope mementos.

JM

Fantasy Island Toys
335 Fairhope Avenue

If there is a youngster in your life, you won't want to miss visiting Fantasy Island Toys.

The store's motto is, "Where Kids Go WOW!" and that is an accurate reaction to the eye-popping stock of merchandise on display. Located in a former hardware store, the façade is colorful and the inventory abundant. Some toys are educational for the junior scientist; some are more tuned into the young Ninja Warrior, up-and-coming athlete, or karaoke singer. There is a plentiful selection of games and books, as well as art supplies and kits. The owners are committed to providing the best possible tools for healthy play.

All summer long, for a nominal fee, children can participate in activity classes such as Science Lab, Paint a Bird Feeder, Dig it Up Dinosaur Excavation, and more. Check the schedule online at FantasyIslandToys.com to register for an event.

One might expect the toys at Fantasy Island to be pricey, but prices are competitive and the selection goes way beyond Wal-Mart. Stop in and see for yourself.

RG

Greer's Grocery Store
75 S. Section Street

There is an old rumor that Greer's was here to greet the Native Americans when they first landed in their canoes. Greer's management denies it. The point is that now and then we all need a downtown grocery store for unplanned and unexplainable urges, including last minute desirables. Bottle of pinot noir? A package of four hard boiled eggs? A bag of extra zesty potato chips? A jar of stuffed olives? Breakfast sausage biscuit with cheese? Or a thirty-pound bag of ice?

You get the point; we have a tried and true grocery store right down town. You may discover a whole section of products made right here in Fairhope, like Betty and Nancy's homemade blueberry and peach jam. As my cousin from Ohio said upon his first visit to Greer's, "Sometimes the everyday things in life turn out to be better than what you went looking for in the first place." Right.

RM

Lotus Bluum
6 S. Bancroft Street

Lotus Bluum is a destination stop for everything to nurture the free spirit, joy in life, and peace of mind. The shop offers a unique variety of services, such as group and private meditations and alternative and holistic approaches to nurturing the body, mind, and spirit.

Kirsten Kelly is an extraordinary massage therapist and Reiki Master offering a full menu of massages, including hot stone and traditional methods to bring a feeling of calm and balance. Kirsten is trained in Thai Massage, NeuroMuscular Therapy, and various sound healing techniques. She can be reached for appointments at 251-599-5943.

Rebecca Salonsky is a psychotherapist specializing in hypnotherapy. She offers psychological counseling as well as regression therapy, including targeted and quantum healing techniques. For an appointment with Rebecca call 251-928-1241.

Step into Lotus Bluum and experience the calm restorative atmosphere. Balance your life; nurture your spirit; feed your soul. Call Kirsten or Rebecca to book a session or find out about group meditations. Unexpected pleasures in a small, Southern town.

RG

Page and Palette
Section Street

Our independent bookstore, wine bar, author event venue, and fun place to hang out and get a cup of coffee or an ice cream is thoroughly depicted on page 41.

Running Wild
214 Fairhope Avenue

Running Wild is a store for runners and walkers of all levels and abilities. The store has been at this location on Fairhope Avenue for almost a decade, helping Fairhopians and visitors set and reach their fitness goals.

The knowledgeable staff's main focus is to be sure you exit the premises with the right pair of shoes to keep your feet, as well as bones and joints, protected from harm as you embark on your fitness mission. Running Wild also carries a line of fashionable, sleek running apparel.

Running Wild holds weekly group three- to six-mile runs at 6 p.m. every Tuesday for all abilities. Once a month, following the Tuesday evening run, stay around for a social hour featuring good food and good times until 8:30 p.m. Wednesday is the ladies only *Wild Tribe* run. Run, walk, or stroll with the kiddos at 9:30 a.m. Saturdays at 6 a.m., there is a regular longer run, again for all abilities. Group runs meet and leave from the Running Wild store on Fairhope Avenue. There is no signup necessary; just show up and RUN!

The store holds training groups for the serious competitor. Train for a 5K starting in July; half marathon training begins in August, and a marathon group begins training in September.

Running Wild sponsors a Grand Triathlon in Fairhope in June and a Jubilee Kids Triathlon, also in June.

The store is an active participant in Fairhope's annual Girls Night Out, held yearly the second Thursday in May. For that event, they offer free wine, free gifts, and free massages.

Stop in the store to check out the shoes and apparel and find out about these events and programs.

RG

For the Furry Friends

Give a Dog a Bone

59 S Church Street, # B

Photo by Ken James

After a hard day rolling in the grass down at the Fairhope pier, and sniffing all the wonderful flowers around the shops downtown, you might want to treat your canine companion to a good wash and shampoo. You have several choices for pet grooming in Fairhope.

If you would prefer to wash your pet yourself, you can stop by Give a Dog a Bone, a DIY pet grooming salon located just two blocks south of the Page and Palette bookstore.

Owner Molly Beasly, a blue water sailor in a previous life, will cheerfully welcome you inside, where you have a choice of one of four large elevated tubs, equipped with blow dryers and accessories. The eleven-dollar charge includes soap and a popular blueberry facial shampoo, brushes, combs, and towels, as well as all the warm water you need.

If you don't want to do your dog's nails, Molly can do it for you for an extra nine bucks. You can be in and out in three shakes of the tail, all clean and nice smelling again, ready for another great day in Fairhope.

Hours are 9-5 M-F, 10-5 Saturday, 1-5 Sunday. They are closed on Saturdays in July.

KJ

South Beach Park

S. Mobile Street by the pier

A nice fresh westerly off the bay, waves lapping quietly on the sands, a beautiful sunset silhouetting sails, a nice walk around some green grass with picnickers and kids playing, a wonderful fountain amidst a great rose garden...how could it get any better? Bring your dog, of course!

Photo by Ken James   South Beach Park, located next to the water fountain down by the pier, is a great place to take a shady lunch break under the trees. You can also go for a jog, have a glass of wine with your girlfriend while watching the sun dip into the cloudy haze across the bay, let the kids romp and chase fireflies, set up a camera on a tripod and capture memories, do a little oil painting in the cool of the morning, have a twilight astronomer's club meeting while letting beach front strollers check out the wonders overhead, show off your restored Model A Ford, fly your drone, have a wedding reception, fly a kite, play a flute or a guitar, practice your yoga or tai chi, join a group for touch football, toss a Frisbee or a ball with your dog . . . well, you get the picture.

In addition, all my dogs have loved investigating all the scents, and meeting all the other dogs of every description walking around the park. There are plenty of disposal bag dispensers, and lots of trash receptacles. Dogs are not allowed on the pier, although they will pull mightily toward the temptation! Before you leave, take a few pictures by the rose garden; the fountain makes a great backdrop. You and your dog will have fond memories.

KJ

Waggy Tail
16 S Church Street

While this shop may seem small at first glance, it impresses with its array of high quality pet foods, leashes and collars, crates and mats, toys and treats, pet outfits, and one Russian blue cat that causes pets and owners alike to prance over for introductions. Jubilee, the cat, delights in peaceful repose after closing hour right in the front window where she can antagonize and then ignore passing dogs. A harmless pursuit, really.

A lovely, fluffy stuffed poodle often leans regally against the wall startling visitors when it belies first impression and stands straight, gently shaking its altogether real blazingly white coat. The poodle, Truman, is a perfect advertisement for Waggy Tail's grooming salon in the back.

Waggy Tail, formerly known as Pet Haven, has been in business as a pet store and grooming business in that location for close to thirty years.

For expert grooming, or even a spa treatment with in-tub massage for your fur babies, come to Waggy Tail. Truman and Jubilee will be glad to meet you.

PP

Lagniappe

Radio Station WABF 1480 AM

Forget your iPhone and other music-at-your-finger-tip devices that play predictable—usually boring—music, and please tune into our very own radio station. You will get the local weather, the local traffic, and best of all in the mornings you will hear the "Swap Shop" hosted by two local legends.

Lori DuBose and her able but mysterious co-host, Mark, handle things quite well. You can hear callers telephone in things they are trying to sell or trying to buy. Antique Singer sewing machine, the type you pedal, yep. Thirty-eight-foot-long shrimp boat with all the trimmings, yep. A 1929 Ford A Model coupe in pristine condition, yep. Quart jars of freshly made blueberry jam, yep. How about a smart yellow lab puppy that will untie your shoe laces? Yep.

Point is, you will hear the community come alive with the things they need and the things they need to sell. My friend, L. Darris Mullins, recently bought a 1993 Ford pickup truck and found a quart of silver dollars, a pair of newish work boots that fit him, and a pocket knife identical to one he had lost thirteen years ago, all under the seat.

I am not saying you will have a similar experience, but you can listen in and share the common thread of humanity doing life together. Finally, and most importantly, to the iconic music. Who else would mix Elvis Presley, Diana Kraal, The Supremes, Dean Martin, The Who, The cast of Cats, Karen Carpenter, Willie Nelson, Simon and Garfunkel, and Elton John all together in one happy bowl of cherry Jell-O? Yep, WABF. Bless their hearts.

RM

Things to Do

Art Wide Open Studio

6B S. Bancroft Street

Becky Kiper opened her Art Wide Open Studio to affirm her motto, *You're Never Too Old to Color.* She works with individuals and groups assuring them, "There are no mistakes—just happy accidents."

Would-be artists of all ages can visit the studio knowing that they will leave with a "masterpiece" of their own creation. Becky provides space for people who are afraid of the blank canvas, tapping into their inner artist.

Visitors to her studio are encouraged to "Relax and have fun. You can't screw this up." Whatever your trepidations, you plunge ahead knowing, YES, I CAN.

You can schedule an event such as a kid's birthday, girlfriend party, or bring some friends there just for the heck of it. The tools are provided, and you may bring your own refreshments. There are open studio hours. Check the website to access the calendar. Schedule a time to visit or just drop by.

Becky tells me, "Art saved me—when you're creating, it is almost meditative."

Can't beat Art Wide Open Studio for that rainy day when you don't know what to do with the kids. For more information, call 251-233-0203

RG

Go Golfing
Lakewood Golf Club
Located on Scenic 98 in the heart of Point Clear

This is part of the excellent Grand Hotel Marriott Resort in Point Clear. Here you will find two challenging Robert Trent Jones Golf Trail courses. Rolling fairways are coupled with tight greens, spring-fed lakes, meandering streams, and classic Southern stands of hundred-year-old oaks. World Class grounds and the site of the 2001 U.S. Open. The Lakewood Golf Pro Shop has all the details. 251-990-6312.

RM

Quail Creek Golf Course
19841 Quail Creek Drive off Hwy 181

Here before you is an affordable city-owned golf course located five minutes away from downtown Fairhope. The course includes well-manicured greens, fairways, and tee boxes. Included are three lakes and forty sand traps. PGA professional

Bobby Hall oversees the regulation 72-par course. Call 251-990-0240.

RM

Rock Creek Golf Club
140 Club House Drive

Designed by world famous Earl Stone, Rock Creek delivers a playable and enjoyable experience for golfers of all skill levels. This is a full-service golf club, with an award winning restaurant atop a charming view. The 6,900-yard course is welcomed by long hitters. Known as a player friendly course, it is favored by locals and embraced by out of towners. Numerous dog legs add to the challenge. Call 800-458-8815 for more details.

RM

Fairhope Community Park
Church Street and Morphy Avenue

This kids' paradise located at the corner of Church Street and Morphy Avenue will charm any child between the ages of two and twelve. Pass through the entry gate designed to keep the little ones contained, and prepare to be impressed by the two-story tornado slide that will have your little ones caught up in a twisting speed ride. The tiled wall of kiddie handprints offers no thrills, but will bring a smile to anyone who has ever received the gift of a tiny hand-printed plate or garden brick. A spherical climbing structure was filled with boys on the day I visited the playground. They were caught up in imaginary play, swinging from bar to bar, far from thoughts of their electronic devices. Soft rubber at the base of all the playground structures keeps nasty injuries at bay. There are more traditional playground equipment features throughout the area, including a smaller twisty tornado slide for the less courageous.

The *piéce de résistance* of the park is the splash pad. Parents and grandparents gather on the many benches surrounding the area to watch their little ones run through the jets of cool, letting out squeals of delight. Two model boats are big enough to climb on and in to stir the images of pirates, sailors, or Noah and his ark. The splash pad is open and running every day except during the chilly winter months. As soon as it's warm outside, the game is on!

Do not hesitate to visit the Fairhope Community Park if you have children with you on your visit to Fairhope. It is a can't-miss delight.

RG

Let's Exercise!

If you are like most of us, you like to walk when you visit a place. This usually comes early in the morning or after a very satisfying lunch. I will start with a short hike first. My starting place is the corner of Section Street and Fairhope Avenue. These are four corners that are the heart of Fairhope. Turn north on Section Street and walk one block until you are at the corner of Magnolia and Section, now cross the street and walk (west) down Magnolia two blocks to North Summit Street. Turn right and start your tour for four blocks; it is there you will pass some new larger cottages and some old smaller cottages.

Most of the way, you will be out on the street, because we don't believe in sidewalks everywhere and also because all the people who live out here drive about nine miles an hour and are familiar with people strolling down the street. You will notice hundred-year-old oak trees shading most of the walk, and for all of us walkers that is very good in the summer. At the end of North Summit, the street turns left on North Street, then south and becomes Bayview Avenue; this is where the walk takes it up a notch and becomes quite a treat. For on your right, just beyond what we call the bluffs, will be Mobile Bay. The homes on the left are more in the grand tradition, each one with a glorious view of the bay. This part of the walk is not so shaded, so wear a hat. But you will notice a nice long green park high on the bluffs, and many of the people who live out here stroll with their pets along about sunset. Now continue south the next four blocks enjoying the different homes and gardens past Magnolia Avenue. On the right is Knoll Park, soon to be the site of a botanical garden; you can stroll in there for a while enjoying some century old virgin trees—maybe the ghosts of some early settlers or even Indians. After a few pleasantries, you encounter Fairhope Avenue and turn left and up the four blocks back through the town, past lots of great shopping, and to your starting place. Caveat: As you may have noticed, there are cross streets between North Summit and Bayview, which means you can cut your walk short at any time or add to it at any time. It is all up to you. This is about a sixteen-block walk, which is slightly less than a mile and should be about a forty-five-minute stroll, depending on your age and agility.

Now to the medium run. I will start you again at the clock at the center of town. Face west down Fairhope Avenue and walk either side all the way down toward the bay about six short blocks to the fountain and the rose garden at the entrance to the pier. Turn left and run the sidewalk through the park. There are two sidewalks, but it is a looping circle, so it is your choice. At the end of the sidewalk, you will find a set of wooden stairs. Take your time! You do not have to run the stairs. At the top, you will find more park overlooking the bluffs. There are also benches to rest, and a sidewalk that runs down Mobile Street.

For the next several blocks, there will be homes along the bluff. Along here, there are some wonderful gardens and nice examples of creative landscaping. Then, after a little walk down an incline, you come to our boat ramp, and the park restarts again. For those who want to sit down and rest, there are benches along here too, and also there are a few fishing piers you may want to stroll out onto. You could even take off your shoes and dip your feet into the bay waters. You might even walk barefoot down the shoreline in the tan beach sand. This area is shaded by some lovely trees—although hurricanes over the years have blown down quite a few, hence, we are planting more for the future.

Now, enjoy the next part and stop and look at some of the statues we have erected here and there. You may notice we have tried to keep everything native along the bay, so the wild grasses you see are the way it was when the Spanish explorers first stepped onto its shores. We don't water the park grasses either.

When you finally come to a large white three-story building— American Legion Post 199—you will have traveled 1.1 mile. You could turn around and retrace your steps, but now everything is on the opposite side, right is left and left is right, and therefore, as my good friend Bargood Kneefall used to say, "Looks the same, only different." Yes, it will look different as you race back to town. Caveat:

There is another way back besides retracing your steps. If you are adventuresome, head into the Fruit and Nut District and zig and zag your way back to the center of town under some welcomed hundred-year-old oaks. It is almost impossible to get lost if you keep turning right and left, right and left. What you will experience is where many of us live. The Fruit and Nut District is named that because many of the streets bear those names. Like Orange and Pecan, or Fig and Kumquat. Here, you will see tiny cute original cottages or some of the newer more up-to-date ginger bread cottages. Overall, this is about a forty-minute run, but it entitles you to say you really worked off lunch and possibly pre-worked off the big dinner you are about to have. Please take a hat and a bottle of water and maybe your camera. You will want all three. One more thing, there are some public restrooms along here and there. The American Legion Post will also welcome you, especially if you stop and have a cold drink with them. They are nice people and will invite you to stay as long as you want. Happy hour starts at three.

Now, to the serious walker and the serious runner. In this plan, we will suggest you start with the medium walk or run as explained above, but as you approach American Legion Post 199, the big white three-story building, a distance of 1.1 mile, you may continue down the sidewalk and south on Scenic 98, which is also known as Mobile Street. After several hundred feet, the sidewalk transposes itself over to the left side of the road, and you are now on the Jill Hall Aerobic Trail. This section is used by walkers and runners and now travels another 1.5 miles down to the Grand Hotel. If this is as much as you want, merely turn around and retrace your steps back to town.

However, if you choose, you can run or walk beyond—and by beyond we mean you can run or walk and follow Scenic 98 on the Jill Hall Aerobic Trail another 10.1 miles from the Grand Hotel ending at the Week's Bay Bridge. At that point, you will have traveled 12.7 miles from downtown. It's up to you to turn around when you are half exhausted.

These are all one-way figures. Double for round trip. Just reverse course. And, yes, everything you saw on the right will now be on the left, and everything you saw on the left will now be on the right. It's a phenomenon that bespectacled scientists from major universities cannot explain. Neither shall we. Enjoy your walk or your run, as you will have friendly company out there doing the same thing you are doing. Oh, yes, one thing more, enjoy the fresh air, someone makes us a new batch every morning. It's free.

RM

Pro Cycle & Tri
510 Fairhope Avenue

Do you want to easily get to some Fairhope destinations that are a bit further away such as the fishing pier, the Fairhope Brewing Company, or the Warehouse and Fairhope Roasting, without the hassle of finding parking? If so, or if walking just isn't your thing, you can rent a bicycle at Pro Cycle & Tri, located just a few blocks down Fairhope Avenue close to the public library.

There, the shop will rent you a nice comfortable but efficient hybrid/commuter bike for six dollars per hour, or thirty dollars per day. The weekly rate is very economical at one hundred dollars. No deposit is required with a credit card. They will adjust the bike to fit before you leave.

You can also pick up a good pair of casual riding shorts or shirts, or a helmet, or a very bright rear blinking light from their collection of riding gear and accessories. Let Katie or Joseph help you with your selection and fit.

The store has a wide selection of all styles of bicycles and equipment, as cycling is understandably popular given the excellent roads and beaches near Fairhope. Of course, they also sell road and mountain bikes of various styles and price ranges from weekend warrior to full-bore competition, as well as commuting style bikes to ride to work or on errands around town. Joseph Bolton, one of the owners, can help you find your correct bike size and make sure it will fit your individual body and tush perfectly—very important if you want comfortable mileage!

The store is enlarging its clothing section and remodeling so that customers can have an easier interface to the service bays. This means you can watch your wheels being built, or your bike tuned up, and the mechanic can show you what that nasty curb did to your rim! Or you can watch them at work and pick up some tips on how to keep your bike in tip top shape.

Pro Cycle and Tri organizes a number of weekly rides from the shop that are open to the public. They welcome you Tuesdays at 6 p.m. in the summer, and also Thursdays at 6 p.m. Both rides average thirty riders or so. Tuesday is a fast ride of about twenty-five miles; Thursday is twenty miles at a social pace. Go to the website at procycleandtri.com for Saturday and all ride descriptions.

Call if you wish to ride, as the schedules do change with the seasons.

The shop also sponsors an amateur triathlon team, the "Gulf Coast Tri," and they support a number of local triathlon and cycling events as well.

So if you would rather be biking than walking around Fairhope, or you need a good bike or some cycling gear, or want to connect with the local tri or bike scene, Pro Cycle & Tri is the place to come in Fairhope.

KJ

Sitting
Anywhere you darn well choose

The art of strolling for a time and then sitting is still practiced in Fairhope—and almost to Olympic standards. First, you should know there are two types of sitting. One is to stop and sit and read something such as a newspaper, a book, your iPhone, or a list of something you might want to do in the future—like wash the car, get a haircut, buy some bananas.

However, the true aficionado reads nothing and looks out into the world attempting to appreciate it all. This desirable individual looks for clues in the faces of passersby, in dogs on leashes, or in pickup truck bumper stickers—or just counting the number of young mothers pushing baby strollers holding cute babies, with toes sticking out.

Obviously, you will need a place to do this and we suggest any sidewalk café for starters. Yes, there are cafés all over town with tables and chairs made just for you. You can nurse that coffee or tea with the best of them. Next up are benches placed around town. Some are in the shade and some are in the sun. You will soon learn to choose the right one for the season. But we must not overlook benches in our parks, some with a great view of the bay, and some with views of our duck pond. Next are a variety of benches, near Julwin's, the Single Tax Colony offices, and even rocking chairs or swings here and there.

I hope you see the point in this. And that is, bistro chairs and benches, and even rocking chairs, are meant to receive us in a resting position, and in that position, we are meant to think.

Herbert Voldenhouse walks to town every day and takes a seat at one of his twenty-three sitting places and just watches people pass by. When asked why, he said this to me and he said it very poignantly, "Everything in Fairhope is unexpected. Fairhope itself is the ultimate discovery." Herbert did stop there and so he continued, "Yesterday, a friend, Osmal Wilson, walked up to and sat down next to me. I haven't seen him since 1999. We talked for an hour and it was delightful. The next day a man I never met before sat down and we discovered we both liked Oldsmobile 88s, peach pie, and Debbie Reynolds. And we had a great time."

I think Herbert put his finger on why sitting is so important. You may discover something, and have a moment to yourself, realizing you are not alone in this thing we call the incredible human experience.

And you thought you were just sitting.

RM

Lagniappe

Jubilee!

"Jubilee," in Biblical terminology, is a time of freedom and celebration. Since we in Fairhope feel that we live in Heaven, the same definition fits the Jubilee that occurs in Fairhope almost every summer on unpredictable dates and always in the middle of the night! Long-timers on the Eastern Shore of Mobile Bay have experienced this phenomenon all their lives. Jubilee is said to happen only two other places in the world, but is well known to be here in Fairhope.

The loud yell of "Jubileeee" comes at the least-convenient hour on a summer night, and locals scramble into the dark with a bucket, scoop net, and any portable light they can find. Within minutes, the sandy bay shoreline will be packed with people picking up fish, crustaceans, and other marine life that swam or crawled ashore, seeking life-sustaining oxygen. The event will last from a few minutes to a few hours. Then the frenzy will stop as quickly as it began!

Technically, a Jubilee occurs when there is a gentle easterly wind, forcing bottom dwelling creatures to the surface searching for oxygen. It occurs when the bay is calm and the air is hot—as warm water holds less oxygen than cold water. It seems to happen after a late afternoon shower, which permits better photosynthesis at night. All elements of tide, wind, water temperature, and salinity combine for the magic moment for sea life to come to us!

Due to the lack of oxygen, the Jubilee-affected fish and shellfish cannot carry out normal muscular activities, such as swimming. They move slowly and seem reluctant to swim even to escape capture. However, few fish or crustaceans die during Jubilees, except for those scooped up by those who rallied out in their pajamas at the loud "wake up" call. There is no way of forecasting when a Jubilee will occur, as only the marine life can feel the phenomenon. But when it occurs, there is little doubt that this extraordinary piece of our history is at hand!!

RMG

How Fairhope's Annual Arts and Crafts Festival Came About

By the summer of 1895, the Fairhope founders were beginning to realize that their farming techniques learned back in Iowa would not work well in sandy soil. For a livelihood, they soon found that their greatest assets were the clays in the nearby creeks and the serenity and beauty of the Eastern Shore. Local crafts became souvenirs for those who came from Mobile and New Orleans to see what these northerners were doing in their single-tax experiment. The Fairhopers built the bay boat "Fairhope" to bring visitors to the Single Tax Colony, and the pottery and artwork of Fairhope caught the appeal of outsiders. Painters and artists also came. Shops opened on Fairhope Avenue that sold wares and gifts.

The Cochran Bridge and Causeway opened in 1927, changing the personality of the Eastern Shore. Bay boats faded out of existence and trucks now delivered goods directly to homes. Visitors could now drive to Fairhope, even though it was a two-hour trip. Likewise, buyers could go into Mobile "shopping" and spending money away from their small hometown. Fairhope was a typical small town with farming, business, and industry nearby. The pottery industry worked alongside potato farms, pecan orchards, and other trades that used clay, sand,

Early 20th Century kiln on Fish River
(built before the power pole was needed!)
photograph by Bob Glennon

timber, and the Gulf for a livelihood. But small businesses in Fairhope were feeling the pinch.

"In the 1950s," said Ms. Barbara Gooden, manager of the Fairhope Chamber of Commerce, "we were trying to find something to pull in tourists." She and her good friend, Ms. Gay Caffee, decided to feature the art work of locals with a festival. In February 1952, the first Fairhope Arts and Crafts Festival was held. The event featured local artists on storefronts and in show-windows—and lasted all week long! The earliest festivals were not all sales; the exhibitors spent four or five hours a day demonstrating their crafts.

By 1966, the festival had opened up to include people from several states and had fifty-two exhibitors and forty-one artists and drew up to 4,150 visitors. In 1967, there were more than 100 displays, exhibits, and demonstrations. There was still no entry fee, but all participants were asked to pay a small commission on their gross sales.

In 1978, the festival for the first time was condensed into three days. This was also the first year that craftsmen were placed on the sidewalks. In 1983, the first prize money was awarded ("Best of Show" received $250), and booths were moved to the middle of the streets. In 1997, the 45th Annual Arts & Crafts Festival was first named one of the top 200 festivals in the U.S. by *Sunshine Artist* magazine.

Arts and Crafts, circa 1978

The festival is now a juried event, with over 600 artists competing for 200 spaces on the streets of Fairhope. Exhibitors from over twenty states are present.

The Eastern Shore Art Center also holds its Arts and Crafts Show at the same time, nearly doubling the size and revenue of the event.

Today, the festival attracts an estimated 220,000 shoppers and enthusiasts over a three-day weekend!

RMG

Occasional Happenings

Eastern Shore Repertory Theatre
On the bluff overlooking the Pier and the Fairhope Civic Center

This is a knock your socks off collection of talented young adult and child singers, dancers, and actors all rolled into one spectacular performance phenomenon. Standing ovations are the norm at the end of each act. I heard the word "Wow!" many times during a most recent show and expect to hear more in the future. Recent and upcoming performances are Disney's *The Lion King*, *Beauty and the Beast*, and *Circus of Dreams*. Exacting rehearsals, professional lighting and sound, incredible costumes, and expert direction deliver award winning presentations. Check out their website for times and dates, or call 251-301-2371.

RM

First Friday Art Walk

One of the hallmarks of community spirit in Fairhope is the monthly (except December) First Friday Art Walk. This event is free and open to all. You'll find many of our art galleries, antique stores, and other locations open from 6 to 8 p.m. on the first Friday evening of the month, for browsing, other special activities, and, at several locations, an appetizer and a glass of wine.

I recommend beginning your tour at the Eastern Shore Art Center at 401 Oak Street, where a new monthly exhibit is launched every first Friday. As you stroll up the street from the art center, you'll find more than two dozen exhibitors displaying their work at the various venues.

As with most street-friendly events in Fairhope, live music can be heard drifting in from several locations. Many restaurants are open for dining options.

Greer's Market stays open for food and wine tastings, and Page and Palette Book Store features book signings and author appearances, as well as live music, during the monthly event.

Fairhope and its people are passionate about art and creativity. Whether you are creatively inclined or just love to appreciate the creativity of others, you will thoroughly enjoy this monthly "happening" in our town center.

RG

Let the Celebrations Commence

Fairhope sponsors and plays host to multiple events in the course of a year. Beginning with the dawn of a new year, right through Santa's arrival in December, mark your calendars for these special Fairhope Happenings.

January The street party begins at 8:30 p.m. on New Year's Eve. Bring the family for this special G-rated New Year celebration, complete with live music, face painting, vendors, and specialty tents. Many of the downtown restaurants remain open, so you can catch a meal or a snack. Stroll the streets for a while and wait for the big moment—a ball drop and fireworks display at the midnight hour. Great family fun.

February Our much-loved community thespians at Theater 98 begin their season with a new play during this month. Founded in 1960, Theater 98 puts on four productions a year—February, May, July, and October. Comedy, tragedy, drama, musical. Come check out the productions in this intimate theater on the corner of Morphy and Church streets.

Mardi Gras in Fairhope kicks off the last Saturday in January with the Mystic Mutts of Revelry—dogs on parade with their proud owners. Immense fun for all. Four other parades, sponsored by the local Krewes, commence on February evenings through the streets of downtown Fairhope. The sidewalks are thronged with revelers hoping to catch a throw or a moon pie while enjoying the bands, brightly lit floats, dancers, and other entertaining spectacles.

Photograph by Rebecca Brunson, Friends of the Fairhope Museum of History

March The annual Arts and Crafts Festival is a three-day event on the third weekend in March, celebrating the creative arts. Fairhope shows off its dazzling abundance of flowers while over 200 vendors offer their wares displayed on the Fairhope streets. The prestigious event attracts more than 220,000 visitors to our town and has been chosen one of the top twenty events in the Southeast by the Southeast Tourism Society. A free event, free parking is available on the city's edges, and a shuttle service will take you to the center of town for a small fee.

April An all-day event at Fairhope Pier Park to celebrate Earth Day is becoming a delightfully popular opportunity to take in the environmental exhibits, and get information on organic gardening, recycling, and energy efficient HVAC systems. Sprinkled throughout all this vital information are booths featuring colorful birds and reptiles for kids to acquaint themselves with.

Food vendors and lively music keep things exciting. The focus is on educating us about keeping our environment healthy. All of this on our beautiful bayfront the third Saturday in April.

May Attention ladies—if you are here in Fairhope on the second Thursday in May, we have a treat for you. Fairhope hosts its **Girls Night Out.** For a $20 fee, you will receive a tee shirt, tote bag, food vouchers, and a coupon book with multiple deals from our downtown merchants. Stroll the streets with your girlfriends and find great specials and giveaways at participating shops throughout the downtown area. Great nibbles and liquid refreshments are offered at most stops along the way.

Summer The lazy, crazy days of summer offer our renown abundance of flowers bursting from every corner as you explore the streets and bay front of Fairhope. Our Pier Park rose garden is in breathtaking full bloom. Thursdays from 3 p.m. until 6 p.m., local farmers and crafters display their goods for sale at the **Farmer's Market** located on the street behind the Fairhope Library.

Summer also brings out the talented **Baldwin Pops**. On holiday evenings: Memorial Day, Fourth of July, and Labor Day, the Pops present a free evening concert on the bluff at Henry George Park. The music begins as the late afternoon sun begins to melt into the bay. The bluff overlooks the fiery sunset as our American flag waves in the bay breeze. The star-spangled setting and stirring patriotic music honors our country and our veterans. Bring a chair and a picnic supper if you wish.

October The **Fall Into Fairhope** celebration commences the first week of October with the coastal **Bird Fest,** an event beginning at Five Rivers Delta nature center on the causeway. The festival sponsors over two dozen trips on foot and by boat to Gulf Shores National Seashore, the Mobile-Tensaw River Delta, Dauphin Island, Bayou La Batre, and many more. The Bird Fest attracts birders from around the continent who revel in the opportunity to explore our diverse and rich natural environment.

The **Bird and Conservation Expo** is on the first Saturday in October on the campus of Coastal Alabama Community College and features hands-on exhibits of sea creatures, as well as raptor demonstrations to engage children and adults alike. At the same time, also on the college campus, the **Festival of Arts** features displays by fine artists and craftspeople.

If you still have some energy, the 5K **Mullet Run** is held on Sunday, along with a one-mile fun run. The Baldwin Pops Band performs a fall concert on the bluff on this weekend's Sunday evening.

<u>November</u> A world class cinematic experience comes to town beginning on Thursday the second week of November. The **Fairhope Film Festival** features over forty award-winning feature films during the four-day event. These films are competition finalists at both national and international festivals. Tickets can be purchased individually or in multi-packages. There are five venues showing the films, all within walking distance of each other. When you are finished viewing a film, the next one on your viewing list is right up the street. Often, directors, actors, and screenwriters are on-site when their films are being shown for a one-on-one experience. The festival has become a major attraction for locals and visitors. Check out this year's offerings at info@fairhopefilmfestival.org

The holiday season commences on the evening of the third Thursday in November with the electrifying **Lighting of the Trees.** Our city workers painstakingly place thousands of tiny white lights in every tree in the downtown area during the dark days of winter. The flowers are still there, but take second place to the bright and light evening drive through town. The official lighting of the trees has become a Fairhope event. Thousands of big and little folks gather in the street, listening to live music and perhaps enjoying a meal at one of the restaurants in town. At the appointed moment, there is an anticipatory countdown and—

voila—the trees all light up with a spontaneous "Ahhh" from the crowd.

December The magical **Christmas Parade** kicks off at 7 p.m. on the first Friday evening in December. Over fifty floats, bands, dance groups, scouts, and other clubs take part in welcoming Santa to town. Throws and moon pies may come your way as you gather on the sidewalk to watch the fun. It all leads up to Santa arriving in all his red-suited splendor. Watching the parade is fun, but watching the faces of the small children on the sidelines is priceless.

Welcome, Santa…hello to another busy Fairhope year!

RG

Live at Five (A Concert Series in Fairhope)
450 Fairhope Avenue

A great new venue for local and regional bands is at Coastal Alabama Community College's Halstead Amphitheater. You can easily check out their web site (Alive at Five) to see which bands are performing Friday nights 5 to 7. While it is not every Friday night, it does takes place about twice a month throughout the year, weather permitting. Admission is usually five dollars and admits you to a green filled with picnic baskets, lawn chairs, and people who feel the music and get up and dance. A fun time for adults and kids alike.

RM

Places to Stay

We will start with the star of the show, the headliner, the top banana, the big gorilla.

Grand Hotel Marriott Resort
Located at One Grand Boulevard, Point Clear

It is here you will discover a self-contained little community. It's where the politicians, NASCAR drivers, Hollywood stars, and famous sport figures soak up the sun and the atmosphere.

Since 1847, the hotel has stood with its arms open to those who seek refinement, incredible food, and a view of the bay that takes the breath away. Three restaurants and a swimming pool are the jewels of this crown. Walk their gardens, sip their mint juleps, and breathe their rarefied air. Steps away you will find Lakewood, a golf course that rivals the best. The ultimate.

RM

Hampton Inn Fairhope
23 North Section Street

A great location for being in the center of everything.

Hampton quality and inside parking. Walk out and turn north, south, east, or west and you will find Fairhope at your feet. A very nice complimentary breakfast inside or out.

RM

Jubilee Suites
557 N. Mobile St.

Some boutique inns boast "a room with a view;" Jubilee Suites can boast "a view with a room." Situated on North Mobile Street just one mile from downtown Fairhope, the property has sweeping bay and sunset views from all angles, and 200 feet of sandy beachfront stretch out before you. One- and two-bedroom suites with one or two baths and full kitchens offer guests all the comforts of home. The clean, fresh, white interiors of the suites do not overshadow those amazing views. Comfortable furniture and balconies with bay breezes make every visit memorable.

Jubilee Suites can accommodate a small wedding, corporate event, or family reunion in the huge kitchen and meeting space in the common area, as well as seven spacious suites for overnight stays. Members of a movie crew made the location their home for a three-month stay while filming here on location.

Yoga and massage are available on weekends. Your pets are welcome with a pet fee. Hors d'oeuvres are served at sunset and you are welcome to bring in your alcoholic beverages. The large kitchen is available for the caterer of your choice.

The inn was acquired in 2018 by Dana and Jim Maloney and the couple has reinvented the property making it a spectacular place to stay for a brief or long-term period. Reserve your "view with a room" today. 251-517-7515.

RG

Bay Breeze Guest House
742 South Mobile Street

Situated on three wooded acres with Mobile Bay lapping at the shoreline is the Bay Breeze Guest House. Turn from the street into a long camellia- and azalea-lined drive to the main guest house and its cottage suites.

Your hosts are lifelong residents of the area and are always available to cater to your needs, answer questions, and simply make sure that you enjoy your visit. They are now into their second decade of providing their guests with tempting food, restful surroundings, and local guidance.

Each of the six guest rooms or suites is furnished with antiques. The guest cottages were originally built to house relatives who couldn't live alone any longer. Now those cottages have become welcoming wood-paneled suites that ooze charm and coziness.

The breakfasts served each morning are meals to remember. Owner Becky Jones has received so many requests for her recipes, she prepared a breakfast cookbook to distribute to each guest.

Outside behind the main house, a brick pathway will lead you to a large patio area where you can sit with your friends (or make new ones) and enjoy bay views and bay breezes. You'll find a dock and a small beach; and the sunsets are spectacular.

You won't be disappointed if you book your stay at the Bay Breeze Guest House, as 92 percent of their business comes from referrals or return visitors.

RG

Cottages of Fairhope
106 South Mobile Street

Looking for a home away from home? There are forty-nine cottages or even desirable furnished homes to choose from and all located all over Fairhope. Choose a one-bedroom to a four-bedroom cottage with a full kitchen and all the amenities. Secret hideaways or big family gathering places. From a few days to extended stays. Phone 251-928-4000.

RM

Emma's Bayhouse
202 South Mobile Street

A quaint bed and breakfast situated right on the bay, Emma's is clean and delightful. You will meet nice people here. Charming is the key word. Service is top notch.

RM

The Fairhope Inn
63 South Church Street

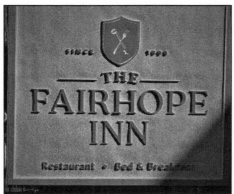

Continuing the hospitality of great American inns of yesteryear, Tyler Kean, owner of the 117-year-old Fairhope Inn has furnished his four cozy rooms with wonderful antiques in the classic Deep South tradition. There are only four rooms here, but each one has its own delightful and warm personality, much like a bed and breakfast, yet with services like a fine hotel. The inn provides a location close to everything downtown, including a nice walk down to the bay. The upscale restaurant on the first floor is a major plus and is reviewed elsewhere in this guidebook. Call for reservations and prices. 251-928-6226.

RM

Barons by the Bay Inn
701 South Mobile Street

This former motel has been newly renovated and boasts its own small but private beach. Good location for walks along the bay or deep into the Fruit and Nut district.

RM

Holiday Inn Express
Greeno Road AKA Route 98

Totally renovated recently, this inn is clean with a great staff. And if you have a craving for fast food, then you are in the right place, as all the biggies are all out here and waiting for you.

RM

Even our avian visitors have classy accommodations.

Not in Walking Distance, but Worth a Short Drive

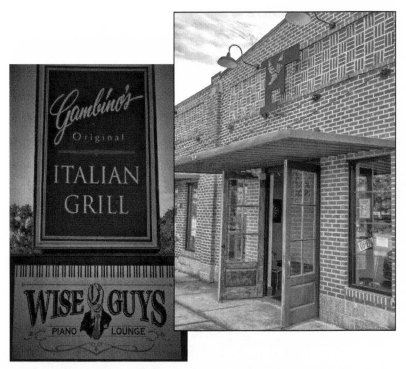

While downtown Fairhope is packed full of great places to eat, shop, sit, and spend the night—or a week or two, there is plenty more to experience close by. Following, we have listed a few drive-worthy places for you. But don't limit yourselves; go out exploring. You might just find your new favorite.

Food and Drink

Agave Cocina Mexicana & Tequila Bar
104 Ecor Rouge Plaza Shopping Center (behind McDonalds)

Tucked behind the local McDonalds on Greeno Road (Hwy 98) is Agave, a treasure to this little town. Agave knows authentic Mexican food and they serve it in style and portions to match. Their salsa, cheese dip, and fresh chunky guacamole are made with original handed down recipes. Upon arriving, you will be treated to a large bowl of chips and salsa and it never ends. The five-page menu is crammed with exciting, authentic delicious entrees. Open seven days a week for lunch and dinner. Agave is a great place for Sunday Brunch.

RM

The Coffee Loft
503 N Section Street

This is the coffee shop that time forgot. Here you will find mismatched chairs, old sofas, and a bulletin board with a hundred and one messages—including all things lost and found and for sale. If Coffee Loft looks like the coffee shop in "Friends," please take our verifiable word, it was here first.

It's a great meeting place for those two-person meetings, to chat about business, sports, politics, or personal issues. I actually heard a conversation about the best places to buy Mardi Gras formal wear at one table. And simultaneously at the next table, I heard three people wondering what breed of dog was that orange and black pile of hair sitting in the front seat of the red Dodge pickup truck parked out front. The thing is, the Coffee Loft is just north of town about a mile and so you will have to drive there. Front parking is limited, so check out the back parking area.

Now on to the coffee. Coffee Loft buys from many coffee bean roasters and then mixes them to find the flavors their customers have come to appreciate. In other words, it's a fine art coffee. The big chalk board lists about fifty coffee drinks and thirty smoothies you could order. And there on the counter top are coffee's partners in crime—pastries. Most of their offerings look like they were locally made, and several look like Ida Bloomquist made it only moments ago in a small cottage a block away. Friendly warning: Astute readers, the banana, walnut, chocolate chip bread is a killer.

RM

El Mexicano
195 Baldwin Square

If you find yourself out doing errands, heading out somewhere on 98, or perhaps returning from the airport in Mobile, and your stomach announces the approaching hour of twelve o'clock, then I suggest taking a break and enjoying a lunch special at El Mexicano restaurant. Located in an unprepossessing building in Baldwin Square shopping center, near the intersection of U.S. 98 and Fairhope Avenue, this family-owned business has been a welcoming stop for locals for a long time.

Inside it is cool and laid back no matter how hot, sultry, and rushed it is outside. You are quickly greeted and supplied with salsa and what some regard as the best corn chips in Fairhope. The lunch specials run from eleven to two and are some of the tastiest and most economical Tex-Mex dishes that can be had anywhere.

El Mexicano is old school in that they still think good food and good service along with plentiful portions and fair prices should win you over. Are they correct? I say "YES"! I had the Mexican plate for dinner recently, and it was just right, very flavorful, so much so that I had no room for desert. Next time I will try the Fajitas; they looked fantastic, and smelled so good.

Dinner starts at three and goes until ten. Margaritas are huge and cold, and there are live Mariachi bands. They are closed on Sundays.

It doesn't seem like much from the outside, but like so many things, it's what's inside that counts. One of Fairhope locals' secrets that needs outing.

KJ

Fairhope Brewing Company
914 Nichols Ave.

The first thing you notice when you walk into the airy, high-ceilinged Fairhope Brewing Company is that instead of mirrors behind the bar, there are windows. Windows across the entire back wall, which allow a view of the large metal brewing tanks and associated gleaming plumbing. These are the tanks where beers with such names as "Take the Causeway IPA" and "Judge Roy Bean" come from.

The brewery has recently increased its floor space by 600 percent to accommodate increased production of their wonderful brews. They brew IPAs, stouts, wheat brews, ambers, blondes, and pale ales. Many of the beers they have on draft are also available in bottles at local grocers, and any beer on tap at the brewery can be put into a thirty-two-ounce can to take home right in front of you while you wait. In addition, they now can ship four of their popular selections. Wonderful! That Judge Roy Bean would go really well with a nice juicy steak!

Although they have no food available in the brewery, you are welcome to bring your barbecue and sit at one of the tables for a good meal with your brew—or maybe that should be a good brew with your meal.

Brian Cane, one of the owners, told me that former mayor Tim Kant has been very supportive of the brewery. I don't know if Mr. Kant likes beer, but if he does, I'm sure by now he knows what a great decision that was.

Brian told me that he thinks the reason their beers come out so well is because they always use premium ingredients, and they have a really good brew master. Have the best people and use the best stuff—yep, that does work!

They have a number of award winners, such as "Take the Causeway IPA," and some truly unique brews as well. I have tried several. My favorite so far is Judge Roy Bean, a smooth, strong, but not overpowering, coffee stout. Brian told me it was the result of an accident; they were aiming at a slightly different result, a more traditional type stout. As far as I am concerned, it was a happy accident.

Speaking of awards, Fairhope Brewing Company garnered the Eastern Shore Chamber of Commerce Small Business of the Year Award in 2017. Way to go!

The brewery hosts music groups on Wednesday evenings and weekends, and, in a twist one might expect in Fairhope, a yoga group meets there the first Tuesday of each month.

Beer is $4.59 a glass, or eight bucks for a thirty-two-ounce can to take home. On your way out, pick up a T-shirt and let your friends know where to get the best beer in town.

KJ

Fairhope Roasting Co.
759 Nichols Avenue

The Fairhope Roasting Co. is located in the rear portion of the building housing The Warehouse Bakery and Donuts. When you sit at a table in the bakery, you can see coffee roasting in action through large inside windows. You might think it is part of the bakery, but in fact it is a separate business. Fairhope Roasting Co. produces several varieties of excellent coffee, which are sold at the Warehouse Bakery and Donuts as well as at Fairhope area grocers.

By the way, the bakery has installed a big shiny espresso machine, so now you can enjoy a wonderful rich cup of real espresso made from freshly roasted and ground Fairhope Roasting Co. beans.

While I was visiting the bakery one afternoon, I decided to stop in at the roaster and speak with someone about their various blends. I met with Chase Sandler, the owner and resident expert. He explained that . . . well, here are his exact words, "We are a small batch roaster for specialty blends and single origin coffees."

He told me how they found their roaster, the machine that cooks the beans, in Hawaii. It was lying dormant at a coffee farm that had switched to macadamia nuts. The roaster was rebuilt in Wisconsin before being shipped to its new home in Fairhope, where it has been busy ever since producing all those great bags of beans.

If you like great coffee from freshly roasted and ground beans (you do, don't you?), don't wait to order online; don't travel or hassle, it is right here in Fairhope! Stop by Warehouse Bakery and Donuts or the various local grocery stores, and try some.

KJ

Gambino's Italian Grill

18 Laurel Avenue
On the corner of Laurel and South Mobile Street

The big sign on the front of the building just says, "Gambino's." For long-time residents, maybe that's 'nuff said, since Gambino's has been a favorite since 1975. For visitors or newcomers, the full name Gambino's Italian Grill says the rest.

The picture that comes to mind is a table filled with pasta dishes, meatballs, and aromatic bread. Well, it's all that and more. Spaghetti and meatballs. Rich, cheesy lasagna. Generous portions of veal or eggplant parmigiana. Cannelloni, manicotti. It's all there. And then some.

If someone in your dinner party is not craving Italian, no problem. There are a variety of seafood and chicken dishes. I recommend the Trigger Fish Oscar. My personal non-Italian favorite is their perfectly prepared prime rib. And the desserts? Mama Mia!

If you're in the mood to linger longer, the Wise Guys piano lounge offers after dinner drinks along with laid-back piano to settle the most persnickety of digestive systems.

They open at 5 p.m. every day.

PP

Grand Hotel Restaurants
One Grand Avenue, Point Clear

Oh my, where to start? First of all, this is the granddaddy of them all. This is an institution and an anchor to the Eastern Shore of Mobile Bay. Accordingly, the Grand Hotel has five restaurants within its walls and situated around the well-manicured and gorgeous grounds. But let's start with breakfast. Yes, there is a small well-appointed coffee shop with great pastry and wonderful designer coffees, which opens at the crack of dawn for those people getting a jump on the day. If you wait another hour, you get to go up the stairs and past the fireplace and walk into the **Grand Hall** for the breakfast buffet governors, senators, ambassadors, and royalty desire when they are in town.

Yes, you can order off the ample menu, but who is that strong to resist an omelet station—made-to-order omelets with eighteen ingredients to choose from. Those privileged few walk down mere steps and load up their oversized plates with fresh fruit, five kinds of meats, crunchy waffles, spellbinding pancakes, flakey croissants, grandmother's biscuits, and Lt. Dan's shrimp and grits.

Well, you get the idea, and that is about only one tenth of what is yours for the taking. You are witnessing a five-star breakfast.

Now onto lunch at the **Bayside Grill**. This is in the same location as breakfast, but now the order of the day is delightful thin-crust pizzas, awesome sandwiches, Royal Red shrimp scampi, scrumptious salads, and some very tempting desserts. Service is fast. Dining is leisurely.

So, you have played a round of golf or gone shopping all afternoon and you are ready for a sunset dinner. Start in the **1847 Bar** for a designer cocktail decked out with herbs and vegetables grown right there on the grounds twenty feet away. After your soothing drink, step down two steps and you will find yourself in the **Southern Roots** Restaurant. This is upscale dining at its best. It is a small menu, but each one is a homerun. Start with the Oysters Grandfeller or Grand Gumbo. For a main dish, the Joyce Farm's Chicken with parmesan grits, garden beans, and cipollini onions proves to be a favorite. There is a scrumptious selection of tender steaks, and a roasted grouper catches most everyone's eye.

Lighter fare for dinner can be found at the **Bayside Grill**, which offers the same menu for dinner as lunch, but now you can have a terrific one-of-a-kind draft beer from their fun beer bar.

I will not go any further without mentioning the **Birdcage Bar** also known as **Bucky's.** This is located steps away and offers the best view of the Mobile Bay sunset, and you can see it while sitting at one of the many outside tables. In the winter; there is a cozy fire pit to warm you. And, yes, the Birdcage has a limited menu with one heck of a great Kobe Beef hamburger. For you romantics, you can dine outside under the stars and watch the moon dance on the water only a few feet away. It makes a perfect ending to a perfect day. Viva Point Clear!

RM

Lickin' Good Donut Shop
110 Greeno Road

This secret is out! The small privately owned donut shop, between Big Lots and Rotolo's Pizza at 110 Eastern Shore Shopping Center at Fairhope Avenue and Greeno Road, has a line out the door every weekend and holiday! It outshines the two big national chains for its donuts, apple fritters, and "kolaches," their term for their own version of sour dough bread with Conecuh sausage inside, for a filling brunch treat. They also have croissants with sausage or bacon, egg, and cheese for a real filler-upper. The colorful sprinkled donuts are on the bottom shelf behind the glass that is marked with tiny handprints from attracting cute kids making hard decisions.

The business is owned by a pleasant, congenial Cambodian man and run by "Le'ake," an always smiling and efficient young lady who knows how to serve customers. Open from 5 a.m. to 2 p.m. daily. Phone (251) 270-8990 to place orders for your church or social event. Very popular.

RMG

Rotolo's
Eastern Shore Shopping Center (corner of Greeno (98) and Fairhope Ave. (CR48)

On the other side of Big Lots, and near Yak restaurant and Lickin Good Donuts, Rotolo's is a pizza and pasta joint boasting recipes passed down from grandma Rotolo. Daily specials vary from Calzone Wednesday to Kids Night Tuesday. Along with an excellent menu and daily drink specials, Rotolo's has an arcade for the kids and trivia games for all. Good food, good fun.

PP

Sunset Pointe
831 N. Section Street

Sunset Pointe is a marvelous seafood eatery just a touch off Section Street at Fly Creek Marina. Outdoor seating is prized in good weather; however, if you prefer to sit indoors, you can still see the fabulous view from the windows. Unique seafood dishes dominate the menu, but carnivores can have their fill of chicken, burger, and skirt steak offerings.

Pete Blohme is one of Fairhope's most beloved restaurateurs, plying his trade with imaginative and creative cuisine at all his restaurants. We love this special place with outstanding seafood— most from our own Gulf of Mexico, served with a spectacular view of Mobile Bay.

They borrowed a nautical term, "bights" to give their menu a seafaring twist with listings under *Small Bights, Bowl and Garden Bights* and *Full Bights,* as well as *Kid Bights.* Each section has its own delights, but my favorite is the *Bouillabaisse,* a seafood hearty soup full of clams, mussels, shrimp, and vegetables in a white wine seafood broth.

Sunset is announced with the ringing of a bell and diners lift their glasses in a toast, to watch a glorious colorful sunset at the close of another perfect day in Fairhope.

RG

Tokyo Sushi & Hibachi
759 Nichols Avenue

If you are craving a sit down hibachi table experience where the chef slices and dices right in front of you then makes a flaming volcano out of an onion, there is only one place to go in Fairhope.

Located next to the Piggly Wiggly in Plantation Pointe Shopping Center, Tokyo Sushi & Hibachi gets mixed reviews from us and other customers. As some have said, "It's a gamble." Service can be slow, but if you by happenstance time it right, or it's close to the weekend, you may luck out and get terrific service with all the bells and whistles. The hibachi offerings rate a "B" to a "B minus" score, while the sushi fares much better, getting a "B" to "A minus" score. They do not like to fire up those big hibachi tables if there are just a few of you, but four adults seems to be the magic number. Prices are reasonable.

RM

Warehouse Bakery & Donuts
759 Nichols Avenue

Just South of Highway 98 on Nichols Avenue, a few blocks away from the Fairhope Brewing Company, you will find Warehouse Bakery & Donuts. They are in the front part of the building occupied by the Fairhope Roasting Company, a coffee bean roasting business. They're a bit off the beaten path, but if you rent a bicycle from Pro Cycle & Tri, Warehouse Bakery & Donuts is only a short ride from downtown Fairhope.

The last time I had croissants this authentic, this good was in Nice, France. Their croissants are the real deal—tender, flaky, buttery, slightly chewy, and so wonderful tasting! They now have brewed-while-you-wait espresso coffee to go with the bakery goods, and they have some very nice coffees in flasks, brewed from Fairhope Roasting Company beans. They also have a very smooth, but quite robust and flavorful, cold brewed iced coffee that is well worth every cent.

There is a good breakfast and lunch menu available: pancakes, fruits and fruit juices, breakfast bowls, biscuits, grits, sandwiches, salads, soups, and even beer on draft and in bottles. They have the excellent brews of the Fairhope Brewing Company, including my favorite, Judge Roy Bean coffee stout, made with coffee beans from the Fairhope Roasting Company. What a nice connection! And what a great combination!

The dining area is roomy and bright, twelve tables or so and plenty of comfortable chairs, with a small private room available also. There is a kids' table with a chalkboard top, and there is a long table off to one side with stools, a sort of "laptop bar," for those who want to work outside the office or maybe tourists who just want to stay in touch while on vacation. You can watch the coffee roasting process through a large window next to the dining tables, and the marvelous aroma while the beans are roasting is unforgettable.

Warehouse Bakery & Donuts offers various bagged beans from the Fairhope Roasting Company for sale on display next to the bakery counter, blends named Fairhope, Warehouse, and Toasted Pecan, as well as others, so pick your favorite on your way out.

They are open 8 a.m. to 6 p.m. Sunday through Thursday, and 8 a.m. to 9 p.m. on Friday and Saturday.

Yes, they are a ways off the beaten path, but once you first visit, you will agree, they are worth the extra effort.

KJ

Wash House Restaurant
17111 Scenic Highway 98, Point Clear

As we advise all our new friends, "Don't be fooled by the outside, you are at the right place." The Wash House is located about a mile south of the Grand Hotel and behind the Punta Clara Bakery. Many of the local food fanatics refer to it as a hidden gem, although from the outside it looks like a Civil-War-era wash

house, and that, indeed, is its origins. Wash house refers to a building where laundry is washed, dried, and ironed. Today no laundry is washed here; instead, the purpose is creating delicious food, and that is why you are here.

The Wash House has a limited menu because of their small size, but what they do offer is noteworthy. Here are some of their best: an outstanding shrimp stack highlighted with fried green tomatoes, a blackened red snapper, an incredible eight-oz. filet topped with crab meat, and the ultimate chateaubriand. But please save some room for the key lime bread pudding, for it is a legend. If you are early for your reservation, pass some time in an intimate bar perfect for light chit chat. Pricey, but a special place for a special evening. Romantic.

RM

Yak the Kathmandu Kitchen
400 Eastern Shore Shopping Center (near Big Lots)

Some say it is Indian, others say it is Nepali; we say it is deliciously wonderful. It has the taste you can find only in the Himalayan Mountains. Which means they use Nepali masala spices which give it the authentic flavors you will find at ten thousand feet overlooking incredible views. Their lunch buffet is noteworthy—just makes sure you get there about 11:30 when it comes out of the kitchen fresh and hot. The dinners are almost the same as lunch but with many more exotic entrees to choose from. Yes, Matilda, the décor may be a little underwhelming, but that is not why you are there. An interesting choice for Sunday brunch.

RM

Shopping and more

Fairhope Furniture Consignment
458A N. Section St.

This shop is not in a realistic walking radius, but you'll need your car anyway because you're going to find something wonderful at Fairhope Furniture Consignment. The showroom is packed with upscale items large and small, and the best part is, you never know what you will find each time you browse. Be sure to look for Sissy, the shop cat who may be snoozing curled up in a comfy corner.

The store features furniture, accessories, antique items, lamps, lighting, candles, china, glassware, art work, rugs, pillows—gently used or brand new. If you are searching for a unique gift for a hostess or graduate, try searching here.

Delivery is available for the larger items. If you can supply some of the muscle, they have access to a fellow with a truck who will haul your merchandise for a reasonable price.

Just a mile or so north of downtown Fairhope, the shop is worth a look.

RG

The Silver Market
Clearwater Circle & Scenic 98

Perhaps you took Scenic 98 today to The Silver Market when you thought of your mother's sugar shell. Now you regret you did not accept the gift of a small lace-trimmed tablecloth and her silver cream pitcher. And since you have recently moved to a neighborhood where your new friends meet for coffee, these pieces are exactly what you might want to accentuate the occasion.

You enter the building into a large room gleaming with sterling silver hollowware and flatware, gossamer white fabrics, and laces from around the world. You feel transported in time as you are surrounded by pristine, storybook Victorian items. The spell will be broken by the entrance of the stunning owner, PJ McAleer, who makes you feel immediately at home in the Victorian atmosphere.

As you wonder how she came to develop this unique setting in Fairhope, she says it all began when she looked forward to her mother's unpacking process of the barrels of china, crystal, and silver after another move when her father returned from his service in the military. This process represented her family's celebration after his long absence. The unpacking meant that soon they would be reunited in the ritual of sitting together in formality at dinner.

Later, PJ began to regard these silver, crystal, and china pieces as important art elements of the material culture which should be preserved. Now she thinks of them as aids to encourage behavior. She sees the culture as disappearing, and perceives the need to help preserve a way of life, instead of family members dashing to eat on the run, "or worse—eating separately from each other." She continues to affirm her mission to bring people together, using her knowledge of the power of antique silver, crystal, and handmade laces to do so.

PJ's academic background was in science and human behavior. Once, as an airline attendant, she had a moment of insight, observing that she moved differently when she wore slacks from when she wore a skirt. She compared that difference to families dashing away to eat as opposed to sitting together at an appointed table with prolonged conversation. She views The Silver Market as "offering tools for emotional togetherness at mealtime." She began to collect silverware during her years, often overseas, as a flight attendant. She would select a particular piece to highlight the occasion when several attendants would meet for dinner. Members of the many area dinner clubs choose The Silver Market when seeking special pieces for their tables.

The age of pieces in the shop ranges from about 1840 through World War I. She specializes in sterling silver, lace, and table linens from circa late 1700s to World War I, with special interest in Victorian and American coin silver, including hollowware and flatware. There are handcrafted lace, wedding veils, ladies' handkerchiefs, christening gowns, and yardage for special projects. These items are housed in antique mahogany armoires and bookcases. French vitrines display an array of gentlemen's and ladies' vanity items. A collection of brilliant period cut glass is found throughout the store.

PJ has recently expanded her collection of antique wedding and christening gowns and laces. She continues a heavy emphasis on Brilliant crystal glass of the period 1880-1916, "the finest examples of the glassmaker's art."

In her jewelry line are freshwater pearls and silver "Baby Bar" and "Beauty" pins, treasures to be held for generations

Work in The Silver Market involves more than sales. On purchasing, PJ vets for quality and condition on all objects. Washing and ironing linens are routine. She remembers laundering an antique 210-inch linen tablecloth.

A large antique cabinet houses hundreds of individual sterling silver flatware pieces. These are available in a wide variety of patterns available for customers who are looking for extra or missing pieces to match their set of silverware.

When asked her favorite piece in the shop, the answer was spontaneous and expected: "The whole pulled together." Her aim is beautifully accomplished. Silverware, hollowware, linens, lace, and glassware are often referred to as accessories—but not by PJ of The Silver Market, who sees them as essential.

JM

Joyce's Hair Salon

119 Lottie Lane
251-510-9905

A vintage cottage, once known as "The Knights of Pleasure Lodge," and which once housed Black children when their Anna T. Jeanes School was burned down in 1952, sits in the Winn-Dixie shopping center. This is Joyce's Hair Salon, formerly functioning as a barbecue restaurant.

Joyce's talents of imagination and artistry were employed in remodeling and redecorating the building for her hair salon, while retaining the original antique fixtures and personality of the

building. Joyce says, "My idea was to offer a cozy atmosphere where my customers could feel at home." The result of the new décor assures the patrons on entering a special, individual experience. A sitting area provides comfortable chairs, brewed coffee, and cookies and candy. Outside on the porch is a swing available for those waiting to be picked up. A ramp leads to the parking area for those wishing to avoid the stairs. Older patrons feel secure and assured, receiving attention and assistance, and can be helped to their cars if needed. Personal touch is the hallmark of Joyce's Salon.

Joyce has been a hairstylist for thirty-five years. Her interest in people has been the motivating factor in her work. She is organized and proficient in her performance. She takes pride in having discovered melanoma in two patrons, which enabled them to seek early treatment. "I love what I do and I have met many wonderful people who have become my friends," she said. Joyce's hours are Monday through Friday, 9-5. Walk-ins are welcome.

Susan Postles is the second hair stylist in the salon. She is a vivacious woman with a quick smile for all and a sense of humor. She, too, has over thirty years of experience in her profession. She says her interest in people is a priority in her work. Susan credits the profession with significant importance in her life. She is a meticulous hairdresser. I was impressed when she was careful to interview me concerning my needs when I was scheduled for an appointment with her. She also took a picture of my hair to ensure her performance would be exact. Her hours are Monday, Tuesday, Thursday, and Friday 9-5.

Steve Wash is the third member of Joyce's Salon. His chosen field as stylist spans thirty-five years. He has been associated with Joyce for ten years. He sees his work as "an artistic venture: the variety and construction of work as fitted to the individual—their color of hair and complexion and shape of face." He enjoys the patrons' interaction, conversation, their travels, occupations, and points of view. He thinks it is very important to follow the patrons' direction and ideas. "Pleasing the patron is paramount," he said. Steve appreciates the theme and atmosphere of the salon because he is an antique collector and dealer. He also participates in karaoke. Like so many individuals with artistic leanings, he has not wanted to be "sealed in an office behind a desk." The styling profession he sees as offering a desirable alternative. He is able to choose his own hours and days of work, allowing the variety in life he appreciates. His hours are Monday through Friday 12 noon to 5, after 5 by appointment.

This is an all-around superb establishment with all members emphasizing excellent performance, liking of and service to people. Make an appointment personally with any of the three stylists, and you'll be in for a gratifying and enjoyable interlude in your day.

JM

Lagniappe

Who's Your Daddy's People?

If you grew up in small-town southern America, you are sure to be familiar with some form of the question, "Who are your daddy's people?" I was born and raised in Mississippi, but I found the same to be true in Coastal Alabama when I moved to Fairhope almost ten years ago.

This question is not nosiness, or even simple curiosity. Southerners take family seriously, and if they can establish that one drop of their blood runs anywhere near your veins, then you are kin.

I don't think I ever got out of a store with a gallon of milk in under thirty minutes—and that's if I was the only customer. Checkout didn't mean just paying for your purchases; it meant getting acquainted and finding out if you might be a hitherto unknown cousin.

"Now, which Pittmans are you kin to?" I would be asked. "What's your daddy's name?" That information would be thoughtfully digested while the cash for the milk lay unnoticed on the counter. Then, as the money was picked up, "Is he related to the Howard Pittman bunch or the Edwin Pittman clan?" That answered, I might be free to leave if another interesting possible relative had come in, or we might move on to my mother's folks.

On more than one occasion I did, indeed, find some relation in common. In fact, while interviewing a woman for a feature story on her historic farm, I was elated to find that my mother's people descended from Pocahontas. I was given a copy of the genealogy records

that proved it. My siblings found it interesting and my children delighted to have a Native American princess as a far, far distant cousin.

Many years later, upon meeting a genetic genealogist working on a family surname project, I was told that not only was my mother not descended from a princess, she had no Native American ancestry at all. Those branches on the family tree had no roots in the historical records.

Similarly, I found I am likely not related to the Irish gentry with a castle in County Cork. Irish gypsies or potato farmers are more likely. My most recent near-royal experience was again on my mother's side. It seems there are McRaes that were the constables of a castle in the Highlands of Scotland, and McCraw is a variant of that family name. DNA, however is lacking that would make that connection a certainty.

Lack of proof either way, however, is enough for the McCraws and McRaes in my acquaintance to spend hours talking about the possibility of us all being family. In fact, the McRae clan in Scotland welcomes us uncertain McCraws to clan gatherings with open arms.

Across the pond, just the same as right here in Fairhope, Ala., and all over the Deep South, clan members greet you with a hug, a smile, an introduction, and a question. "Now, tell me, who are your daddy's people?"

PP

Bye Bye

You came, you sat a spell on the porch, and now it's time to pack up and leave. I think we should all stand for a rousing rendition of the Fairhope anthem. Yes, there really is one. Penned in 1917 by a couple of really enthusiastic locals, it goes like this:

> There's a verdant shore by the waters blue
> Where we dearly love to stay.
> There's a village fair, and we long to be there
> On the banks of Mobile Bay.
>
> There's a winter cold in that sunny clime
> Where the sweet magnolias bloom.
> But the gentle breeze thru the tall pine trees
> Fills the valleys with perfume.
>
> On that sandy beach with its shady shore
> We can wander gay and free.
> Or rest in the shade by a fair sweet maid
> 'Neath the green magnolia tree.
>
> Fairhope, Fairhope, Down on Mobile Bay.
> Fairhope, Fairhope, There's where we love to stay.
> Down where the roses are blooming,
> Down by the waters blue,
> Fairhope, Fairhope, I love you.

Contributing Writers

RMG—Robert (Bob) Glennon enjoyed a career in international business before returning to the Mobile Bay area to write non-fiction stories and historical documentaries. He is an independent scholar and public speaker on U.S. history topics. He and wife, Rita, now live in Point Clear. Website: RobertMGlennon.com.

RG—Rosanne Gulisano is a transplanted Midwesterner who found her Utopia in Fairhope. She is a Southern girl trapped in a Yankee body. Rosanne is a promoter of memoir-writing—facilitating workshops and writing groups, and ghostwriting life stories. She is honored to be a member of the Fairhope Writers Group. Contact her at lifestories10@aol.com

KJ—Ken James is a boomer from the windswept plains and prairies of Kansas. He spent most of his life working hard, playing just as hard, and looking to see what might be over the next hill. Join the Navy, see the world? Yeah, been there, done that, found out the questions are always the same, but it's the answers that are so interesting. Ken came to Alabama after retiring from the USN and ended up in Fairhope after hurricane Ivan created a shortage of deep sailboat moorings elsewhere. Ken hopes to always be climbing the next hill.

RM—Ron Meszaros is an avid gardener, and enjoys post-war British films. Ron is an award-winning screenwriter, and is the author of two novels. His plays have been produced in San Francisco, Los Angeles, and New York.

JM—Jule Moon, a Southerner, is the author of *Sherds: A Memoire*, presented in short stories and poems. The book is reflective of her background in journalism, paleontology, archeology, and psychiatry and the influence of English, French, and American writers, as well as the importance of family and friends.

PP—A former journalist, columnist, and editor from Hattiesburg, Mississippi, Phyllis Pittman came to Fairhope nine years ago and fell in with a gang of pencil totin' fiction writers and hasn't looked back. She has published one children's book, *Pony Tales; Night Mischief*, and co-authored an anthology of short stories with the Fairhope Writers' Group. Her first novel, *The Trouble with Grits*, was a William Faulkner/William Wisdom finalist. Website: phyllispittman.com. Contact her at phyllis@phyllispittman.com

JW—Joe Worley is a retired Air Force OSI Federal Law Enforcement special agent and security professional providing services to two Fortune 500 corporations. He is currently writing away his retirement by authoring memoirs and novels. He is the author of *Scandal in a Small Kentucky Town.*

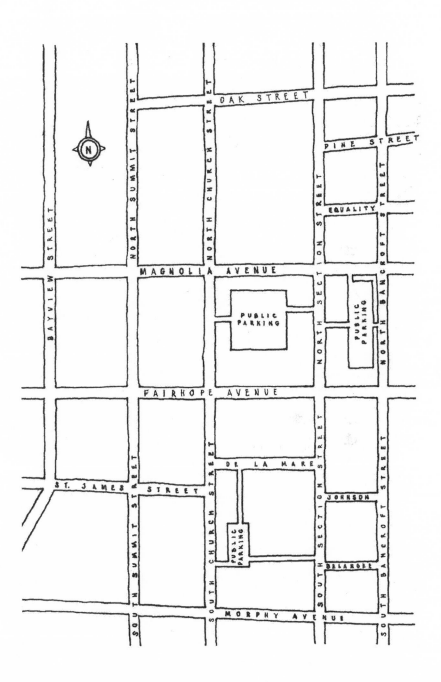

Made in the USA
Lexington, KY
09 December 2019